The Siege of Rhodes

NANAMI SHIONO

Translated by
Carolyn L. Temporelli, Wilburn Hansen and Steven Wills

Published by Vertical, Inc., New York.

Originally published in Japanese as *Rodosuto Koboki* by Shinchosha, Tokyo, 1985.

ISBN 1-932234-32-2/978-1-932234-32-9

Manufactured in the United States of America

First American Edition

Vertical, Inc.
1185 Avenue of the Americas 32nd Floor
New York, NY 10036
www.vertical-inc.com

the siege of Rhodes, however, were cannons put to serious use. Moreover, the battle at Rhodes was a confrontation between the Order of the Knights of St. John, a typical product of the medieval world, and the "modernized" army of the Turks. The knights of the order not only had to be of noble blood, but devoted their lives to Christ as monks.

Leaving aside whether or not this battle opened or closed the curtain on a particular era of history, its defining characteristic was the youth of the men who waged it. The protagonists on both sides at the siege of Rhodes were in their twenties. The Ottoman Sultan Suleiman I, later revered as "Suleiman the Magnificent," was twenty-eight years old. Representing the Order of the Knights of St. John, Jean de la Vallette-Parisot was also twenty-eight, Giambattista Orsini was twenty-five, and Antonio del Carretto had just turned twenty.

The encyclopedia explains the Italian word *cadetto* as follows:

> The term originated in the Gascogne region of France and spread throughout the rest of Europe during the medieval period. It referred to the second and subsequent sons of a feudal aristocratic family. Under the system of feudal estates, it was customary for the eldest son to inherit the estate and all assets, so his younger brothers had to make their own fortunes as clergy or as soldiers. This original meaning of "second or younger son of nobility," though, has disappeared in modern usage, and only its military connotation survives. Now the term is used for students in military or naval academies, that is to say, candidates for an officer's commission. French *cadet*, English *cadet*.

The following is a tale of three young *cadetti* who lived at the beginning of the sixteenth century. It was an era when the nations of Western Europe were establishing centralized states similar to the Ottoman Empire's in order to resist the advance of that empire. Half a century had passed since the fall of Constantinople.

Social change often goes hand in hand with changes in military technology. The power of cannons was demonstrated during the siege of Constantinople and transformed the nature of combat thereafter. Not until

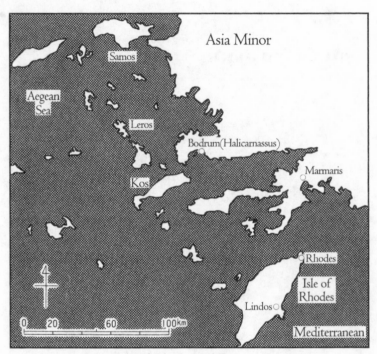

Isle of Rhodes and Environs

Chapter One

The Ancient Isle of
Blossoming Roses

Arrival

In April of 1522, a single, large sailing vessel made its way north with the Isle of Rhodes, aglow in the setting sun, visible on its starboard side. Rhodes rested upon the sea like a long nut stretching from north to south. From the sea there was no sign of human habitation, perhaps because Rhodes's western coast was not blessed with any good harbors offering shelter from the overpowering northwesterly winds that blew through the Aegean Sea between spring and fall. The soft light of approaching sunset washed over nothing but the thick stands of trees, the craggy faces of rocks, and the expansive, uninhabited beach.

Skillful operation of its sails allowed the Genoese merchant ship to make progress despite headwinds. This journey to the Orient had been at the behest of the Order of the Knights of St. John, based on Rhodes, who had hired it to carry ammunition and wheat to the island. After loading ammunition purchased in Milan and leaving from the port at Genoa, it had stopped in Naples. It also stayed briefly in the Sicilian port of Messina, but only to purchase wheat. Ships piloted by Genoese sailors could easily handle a month-long voyage without making a call at port. They could therefore reasonably sail with their specialized cargo directly from Messina to Rhodes without stopping by Crete, which was controlled by the Republic of Venice.

The main cities of Crete were all concentrated on its

northern shore, and a ship could not traverse those waters without drawing the attention of the Venetian naval patrol. To avoid unnecessary trouble with the Venetians, they had to take a long detour around Crete's southern coast and then cut north and head for Rhodes. The Republic of Venice intended to uphold its goodwill treaty with Turkey and maintain a position of neutrality, unlike the Order of the Knights of St. John, which had ignored the Ottoman Sultan's order to surrender and were preparing for war.

A young man named Antonio was aboard ship, accompanied by his valet. He was the second son of the Marquis del Carretto, lord of the Finale Estate near Genoa. He had curly, dark brown locks, and dark brown eyes that made his pale forehead especially conspicuous. He had a calm demeanor and spoke infrequently. This seemed unusual for someone so young, but not so much that it made anyone uncomfortable during the month he had shared the captain's table as guest of honor. The ship's crew and the other passengers, all merchants, quickly grew accustomed to this young man who always had a book open or gazed quietly at the distant horizon.

Antonio del Carretto always wore the uniform of the Order of the Knights of St. John. It was all black except for a white cross embroidered on the chest, and was both the everyday clothing and the clerical robe of the knights of the order. Though he was clad entirely in black, the graceful curve of his legs revealed the twenty-year-old's youthfulness.

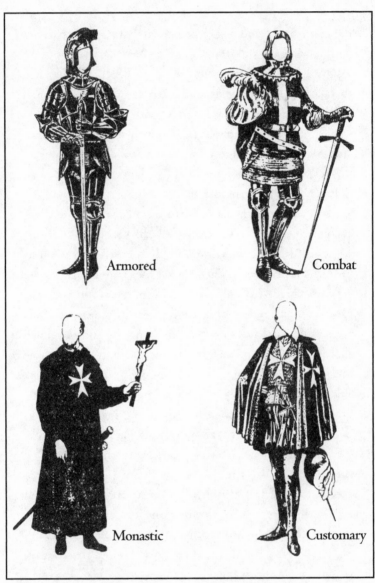

Attires of the Order of St. John

There was a great fluttering of the sails and the ship changed course. The sailors sprang into action. Since they were coming into port with the northwesterly winds at their backs, they had to slow down by replacing the triangular sail with a smaller one and furling the lower half of the square sail.

By then, a shoreline shrouded in lavender mist was visible on the port side of the ship, which had turned hard to the right. That land stretched far to the east. It was the southern shore of Asia Minor—Turkish territory. Both Rhodes and, further to the east, Cyprus were positioned on the front line where Islam and Christendom collided. The distance between Rhodes and the southern extreme of Asia Minor was no more than eighteen kilometers. Since the port of Rhodes in the capital city was located at the northernmost point of the island, the captain of the ship once again turned the rudder starboard as he took the ship around the cape that jutted out from the northern shore.

Winds subsided at dusk in the Mediterranean. Knowing this, sailors embarked in the morning, when gentle breezes began blowing, and paced their journey so as to pull into port at sunset, when the winds grew calm. Incoming ships crowded the port of Rhodes at that hour. The Genoese ship slowed down as it drew near the outer fortress, and the crew collapsed all of the sails once they had passed it. Theirs was a merchant ship, so they didn't enter the rectangular port, named after St. Nicholas, that was protected by the fortress. That was a military port reserved for war galleys, the most common warships of the period. Merchant ships had to bypass it and enter the merchant port that lay beyond.

The flag of the Order of the Knights of St. John, a white cross on a field of red, flew from the Fortress of St. Nicholas, which faced the opposite shore and boasted a long embankment protecting the military port. Atop the embankment, windmills stood in a neat row and made a pleasant sound as they turned. On many islands in the blustery Aegean, the winds were harnessed to grind wheat into flour. Antonio, however, was born and raised in the shelter of the mountains near the Genoese coast and was not familiar with the strong northwesterly winds known as the Mistral. The rows of windmills were a new sight for him, but he was observant enough to notice that they had been placed as close together as possible to protect incoming ships from the wind.

A tugboat pulled the ship into the vast semicircular port, which had a walled perimeter recessed just enough for ships to dock. The massive wall, rising straight up from the dock, had a total of five open gates, each protected by a round, sturdy tower. Another embankment with windmills stretched off into the distance at the wall's edge so that, other than the small waterway needed to let ships in and out, the port was almost completely sheltered from the wind.

Dozens of ships were anchored in the harbor, from merchant galleys that used both sails and oars to plain sailing ships. There were so many that, without the guidance of the tugboats, it was hard to tell where to drop anchor. The ships were tied together, the larger ships facing sideways and the smaller boats with their sterns turned out. The Genoese ship docked alongside the port's first pier on the right side.

The piers were full of people busily loading and unloading cargo, perhaps because the setting sun meant the gates would soon be shut. A group of Turkish slaves bound together by chains listlessly carried a large sack past a group of native Rhodian Greeks, and then past some Western European merchants, whose long robes made them immediately recognizable. Knights wearing armor adorned with white crosses on red breastplates sped between the two groups.

Antonio was standing on the ship's stern, taking all this in with a sense of wonder, when the captain approached and said, "Your welcoming party has arrived." Casting his gaze down upon the pier, Antonio saw two men dressed exactly as he was.

The French Knight

One of the two men showered Antonio with trite but good-natured greetings in Italian. He was a member of the Italian division that Antonio would join, and spoke warmly of a time when Antonio's uncle, the former Grand Master Fabrizio del Carretto, had been in the last years of his life and had treated him kindly. He added that the knights of the Italian division were absolutely delighted to welcome another member of the illustrious del Carretto house to the Isle of Rhodes. The knowledge that he was considered a stand-in for his uncle brought a wry smile to Antonio's lips. The second man, meanwhile, just kept his gaze fixed on Antonio and only opened his mouth when it seemed that the Italian knight had finished talking.

"My name is Jean de la Vallette-Parisot," he said in French. "I serve as the private secretary to the Grand Master." As Antonio gave his own introduction, he thought to himself that this Frenchman, who was no more than seven or eight years his senior, seemed to be acutely conscious of his own nobility.

La Vallette was thin, but he was a tall, handsome man whose wiry physique projected force. The sharp lines of his cheeks, although still radiating youth, seemed to have been carved with a sharp blade and created a very dignified impression. The gleam in his narrow, almond-shaped eyes never wavered from whomever he was looking at. Yet his demeanor, more haughty than graceful, never made others feel uncomfortable; he kept his arrogance within acceptable limits. Even upon first meeting, one could sense that this young man from an illustrious household in Auvergne was a breed apart. Antonio felt he was looking at an exemplar of the "chaste knight" that, although now rare in Italy, had once drawn the praise of all Europe.

"Since you are to meet with the Grand Master, I will come to the Italian quarters tomorrow morning to escort you," said La Vallette. With that, he turned and walked away.

Leaving his valet behind with the luggage, Antonio followed the Italian knight through one of the gates and entered the city. The streets in town were paved with small stones, which felt the same against the soles of his leather shoes as those of the small towns in Italy. The vulgar energy emanating from shops crammed together on both sides of the street, however, felt more Oriental than European. There was a large building of clearly Gothic-influenced design just off an open square at the end of the street, but perhaps because it was constructed from soft, sand-colored stone, it gave the impression of not being entirely Western. The flag of the Order of the Knights of St. John flew atop the towers on either side of the entrance to this magnificent building, which served as the order's hospital. The Knights of St. John, unlike the Knights Templar or the Teutonic Knights, were originally a group devoted to healing the sick.

Even on Rhodes it was customary for buildings to bear the crest of their builder, as in Western Europe. The Italian residence, where Antonio would spend his first night, bore the crest of the del Carretto house above the front door.

The knights' quarters—for the Italians, but also for the divisions from Auvergne, Provence, Ile-de-France, Aragon, Castile, England, and Germany—necessarily varied in size and appearance, but all possessed a similar interior design. There were stables, an armory, a barn, and valets' bedrooms on the first floor. The second floor, which could be reached directly by a staircase from the inner court, had a meeting hall that also served as a dining room, and was encircled by a number of rooms. These were the knights' chambers, where they were required to reside during their first year on the island. In subsequent years the knights were allowed to live in the city. The third floor was an Arabic-style rooftop.

While the design of the knights' quarters was similar to that of a Western monastery, the atmosphere was somehow different. The knights used only the most exquisite utensils, made from silver and engraved with each knight's family crest. The beds lining the rooms were covered with black velvet, each with a crest beautifully embroidered in silver thread. The light hempen sheets were often embellished with the knights' heraldic crests.

Antonio was not the only guest that night in the Italian residence. The other was not a noble. He was from Bergamo, a town in the north of Italy under Venetian rule. Gabriele Martinengo was an engineer with expertise in the construction of castle walls. The Genoese ship that brought Antonio here had briefly stopped in the shadow of a deserted cape just before sailing around the southern shore of Crete. The sole purpose had been to rendezvous with Martinengo, who had fled the island in a small boat.

Antonio fell into the healthy sleep of the young as

soon as his head hit the pillow, fully unaware that Martinengo, a man well into his forties, would become a close companion for the duration of his time on Rhodes.

A First Encounter

The next morning, Antonio practically shivered at the sight of the island's brilliant profusion of colors, something he hadn't noticed when he'd arrived at dusk the night before. Even Antonio knew that Rhodes meant "blossoming roses," yet the lush roses of antiquity were not as striking now after the passage of some fifteen hundred years. In their place, the magenta of bougainvillea, the crimson of hibiscus, the red and white of oleander, and the yellow of lemons seemed to radiate from a background of deep green. He imagined that the flowers of the almond tree, white as snow, had probably blossomed throughout the island until early spring.

The air was mild. The winds that blew so strongly at sea grew softer within the walled city. A gentle breeze always drifted through every alley, immediately carrying away any hint of perspiration. The sky was so blue it looked as if it would rub off on your finger if you pointed at it, while the deep green of the cypress trees stood out in sharp contrast. The island produced building stones primarily the color of sand, which was probably why most buildings in the city were a soft yellow. The stone surfaces of the buildings were exposed, yet this didn't seem unrefined. This was a sun-drenched island in the south, after all.

In the time of ancient Rome, the island was home to an academy of philosophy that was as admired as the school at Athens. Tiberius, who became the second Roman emperor, visited the island to study as a young man, as did Cicero, Caesar, and Brutus. But attaining an education clearly hadn't been their only objective. No ancient race of people was more sensitive to beautiful surroundings than the Romans.

Antonio left the Italian quarters with La Vallette, who had arrived to escort him. That morning, rather than wearing the short, black Western-style manteau he had worn during his voyage, Antonio wore a black robe, embroidered with a white cross on the back, that reached down to his feet. Although this was a southern country, the rule was to wear long robes. Thanks to the refreshing breeze, the knights' robes fluttered in the wind and were not uncomfortable in the heat.

A gently sloping stone-paved road led from the western side of the hospital to the Grand Master's Palace. This road had come to be called the "Street of the Knights" since residence halls for knights from every nation within the order lined both sides of the street. There were those for Italy, Germany, Ile-de-France (normally called simply "France"), Spain (which housed knights from Aragon and Castile), and finally, Provence. The English quarters sat facing the hospital, while the residence of the Auvergne division was close to the shipyard; since neither of these was very far away, one could say that all of the order's most important buildings were located in the same neighborhood, centered around the Grand Master's Palace.

When they had climbed to the top of the "Street of the Knights," they saw a church dedicated to St. John to the left, the most important church for the order. Opposite the church was the front gate of the Grand Master's Palace. It was a perfectly fortified gate, furnished at its highest point with a parapet and protected by two magnificent circular towers. They walked through the gate and came to an entryway seemingly large enough to accommodate a company of soldiers, from which they saw a wide courtyard bathed in bright sunlight. The French knight walked into the courtyard, first passing a staircase originating at the left side of the entrance. Antonio followed.

The courtyard was paved with flat stones and had wells in two corners. Small, narrow windows in the western style had been cut into the surrounding buildings, while sand-colored stones and southern-style arches shading the corridors from direct sunlight made the space seem less imposing. On one side of the courtyard, a broad, open staircase made of stone led directly to the second floor.

La Vallette and Antonio had climbed a few of the stairs when they noticed a man above them. His figure was framed by an arch held up by thin, round pillars. Antonio halted instinctively when the man at the top of the stairs began a slow descent toward them.

Steel armor shining like silver covered the man's tall, slender frame. His breastplate bore the order's white cross on red. In his right hand he held a helmet plumed with white feathers, while his left hand rested on the hilt of the long sword at his hip. Dressed in high battle uniform, he looked ready for combat.

His wavy, flaxen hair was cut short at the nape for ease in donning his helmet, and the color of blood was faintly visible underneath his lightly tanned skin. His eyes were ashen with a tint of light blue, and he cast those eyes, filled with ironic humor, towards Antonio.

Antonio had never before seen such a beautiful figure. The young man stopped four or five steps above them; his clanking armor fell silent. He turned to La Vallette and said in French:

"Is he the newcomer?"

The blunt delivery nearly made Antonio laugh, but the French knight at his side replied in a tone that was far from amused: "This is Lord Antonio, the nephew of Fabrizio del Carretto."

The young man with the bluish-gray eyes laughed cheerfully when he heard this, and said, "So you're also part of the replacement contingent? I'm Giambattista Orsini. You'll probably suffocate cooped up all the time in the knights' quarters, so feel free to pay me a visit from time to time."

He then continued down the stairs, leaving behind only the sound of clanking steel. Antonio turned to watch him go. The sight of the knight's long crimson cloak, trailing behind him, embroidered with a white cross, long remained etched in his memory.

La Vallette stopped when they reached the top of the stairs, as if deciding it was now time to speak. He turned his sharp gaze on Antonio and began, "Sir Orsini is a problematic member of the order. It would be one thing if he concealed his shortcomings, but he openly flouts the order's three principles of poverty, obedience, and chastity. Nonetheless, he is a member of the noble Orsini family, with strong connections to the Vatican. What is more, he is a descendant of the fifth Grand Master. The current Master cannot discipline him though he may wish to do so." Yet La Vallette didn't neglect to add: "When it comes to valor in the face of the enemy, Sir Orsini is second to none. He plunges into the fray as if he were immortal. Even among the Turks, his bravery is considered incredible. He is thought to be the one heathen pardoned by Allah."

Antonio's meeting with Grand Master Philippe Villiers de L'Isle-Adam was uneventful. The Grand Master, from an illustrious household in Brittany, appeared to be a little over sixty and looked like what La Vallette might in thirty years. Only, the twenty-eight-year-old knight from Auvergne seemed to surpass the Grand Master in tenacity, almost to the point of fanaticism.

As Antonio was about to leave, the Grand Master suddenly addressed him with a faraway look in his eye: "Your uncle was my comrade in arms forty years ago, when we fought to resist the onslaught of the Turks."

He was referring to the battle of 1480, when the Knights successfully defended the island from a massive army sent by the Ottoman Sultan Mehmed II. The Christian world was delighted with the results of that siege. The Turks' streak of triumphs since the fall of Constantinople had been broken by the order, whose reputation soared overnight. Fabrizio del Carretto and Philippe de L'Isle-Adam had been younger than Antonio was now.

His meeting with the Grand Master over, Antonio bid farewell to Secretary La Vallette and followed another knight through successive rooms, then down the left vestibule staircase and out onto the street. What stayed with Antonio after he left, far more than the impression the Grand Master had made, were the words carved into the walls of the rooms he had passed:

FERT FERT FERT

Latin for "endure."

Though few manifested Orsini's level of indifference, the knights on Rhodes by and large did not seem to be "enduring" the order's three vows—poverty, obedience, and chastity—save for the obedience. What, then, he wondered, needed to be endured? And how did they endure it?

Antonio had stepped out onto the "Street of the Knights" but did not move. He stood for a moment, feeling through his soles each stone that paved the street.

Chapter Two

The History of the Order

of the Knights of St. John

The Crusades

In the mid-ninth century, when Jerusalem was still under Muslim control, a wealthy merchant named Mauro erected a building that was to serve as both a hospital and an inn for Western pilgrims to the Holy Land. He was from the city of Amalfi, which was active in the Mediterranean even before the other coastal Italian city-states of Pisa, Genoa, and Venice. The crest that would later become that of the Order of St. John, an irregular cross with eight points that is still used today, was originally the crest of Amalfi.

It seems that at some point, however, the Italians in Amalfi lost the control of this organization, which was not yet a knightly order, and leadership came to rest in the hands of Frenchmen from the region of Provence. Around the time of the Crusades, a man from Provence known only as Gerard skillfully managed the hospital and inn that Amalfian merchants had founded.

Gerard's efforts were rewarded in 1099 when the first Crusade resulted in the conquest of Jerusalem. Now that fellow Christians controlled that city, the organization that took St. John as its patron saint was able to advance, in the words of historical sources, "to within a stone's throw of the Church of the Holy Sepulcher," in other words, to the center of Jerusalem. Four years later, Pope Paschal II formally approved the group as a religious order devoted to worship, combat, and treatment of the sick. From that point on, it became known as The

Order of the Knights Hospitaller of St. John.

In 1130, Pope Innocent II gave the Order of the Knights of St. John a military flag featuring a white cross on a field of red. The order decided to use this flag in combat and to keep their old flag, a field of black with an eight-point cross, for peacetime. The importance of having a military flag lay in the fact that the order, originally devoted to healing the sick, was gradually militarizing. In 1119, the Order of the Knights Templar was established as a religious order devoted entirely to warfare. Then, starting with the Teutonic Order in 1190, the other major knightly orders were established one after another. The Christians in Palestine, who had taken the Holy Land by force, felt compelled to defend it with force.

The behavior of secular warriors, however, was not acceptable amongst these knightly orders, which were conceived with the intention of uniting the values of monasticism and chivalry. The knights had to relinquish their worldly status and it was their sworn duty to observe the same vows as monks: poverty, obedience, and chastity. Having a wife was forbidden. They were essentially warring monks.

Although it had been little more than a mob, the army of the First Crusade had successfully taken the Holy Land. As a response to changes both in the crusading armies and among the kings and popes in Western Europe during the Second and Third Crusades, the Order of the Knights of St. John took on an even more militaristic character.

In medieval Europe, it was said that those who devoted themselves to warfare and the protection of others had to have "blue blood" running through their veins. The Order of the Knights of St. John, whose members had always worn the black mantle regardless of whether "red" or "blue" blood coursed through them, now started making clear distinctions between the brothers who used the sword to defend Christians from heathens, and those who used the arts of medicine to heal the infirm. Those devoted to healing, even though they belonged to the same order, no longer received the rank of knight. Furthermore, the highest-ranking member of the order, who had previously been called nothing more than Governor, was now referred to as the Grand Master. This signified the order's continuing transformation into a military organization.

Nevertheless, the Knights of the Order of St. John, who had transformed from "servants of the poor" to "warriors for Christ," managed to maintain a solid *raison d'être* for two centuries, from 1099 to 1291. Power struggles caused rifts among the various knightly orders, so it is fair to say that a united front was seldom raised, but the military strength of the knights was indispensable for the Christian forces in Palestine. Knights participated in every major battle, and it was not unusual for their valiant efforts to turn the tide of combat. The history of the Crusades cannot be written without mentioning their contribution.

At that time, the military strength of the Order of

St. John that could be immediately deployed consisted of only around five hundred knights and roughly the same number of mercenaries. The members of the order were highly organized, however, and their fighting spirit, which arose from their abandoning secular ambition in favor of devotion to God, far surpassed that of the weakly organized Crusaders in Palestine.

After 1187, when Jerusalem once again fell into Muslim hands, the knights of the religious orders were the only ones who could match the fanaticism of the Islamic forces in the numerous battles that ushered in the end of the Crusades. The Islamic forces fervently believed it was Allah's will that Christians be driven into the Mediterranean, and so viewed all battles waged in that aim as part of a holy war. At the time, it was not King Richard, but rather the knightly orders, led by the Knights of St. John, the Knights Templar, and the Teutonic Knights, who fought with the hearts of lions.

Furthermore, the knightly orders had a dependable financial foundation envied not only by the leaders of the Crusader armies in Palestine, but by the kings and feudal lords of Western Europe. It is a demonstrated fact of history that money tends to accumulate wherever the name of religion is invoked.

Patrons had good reason for making donations to religious bodies, and the patrons' kin had no choice but to consent. This was particularly true in the case of medieval knights, since they were sacrificing themselves to fight the enemies of Christ in the distant land of

Palestine. This, at the time, was the highest possible calling. Because the brothers were not permitted to take wives, there was also no danger that the gathered riches would dissipate. Income in the form of donations had the advantage that it continued to accumulate as long as the religious order continued to exist.

Members of orders such as these tended to manage their finances skillfully, and it was common for their wealth to grow steadily. The orders' success was brief, but the economic power of the Knights of St. John, in both property and assets, stretched far and wide throughout Europe, although they were not as blatant in their financial dealings as the Knights Templar, who even dabbled in high-interest money lending. The splendor of the knights' armor was in no way inferior to that of the kings and lords of Europe, and their fortresses were magnificent enough to make the King of Jerusalem envious. At the hospitals of the Teutons and the Order of St. John, each patient was given white bread and high-quality wine and supplied with free sheets and nightclothes.

The knights of the religious orders had developed mental strength and bravery under these ideal conditions, which made them, in the words of the Arabs, "a bone stuck in the throat of Islam." The importance of these "Christian soldiers" was of course recognized locally in Palestine, but also in Western Europe, and even by their enemies. They were willing to fight to the last man; their ferocity came from the strength evinced by those who, though perhaps not satisfied with themselves, are at least convinced of the reason for their being. The years up to 1291 were the golden age of the knightly religious orders. Without their courageous resistance, the expulsion of the Christian presence in Palestine, long hoped for by Muslims, would have occurred much earlier than 1291.

The Refugee Years

In April 1291, a great army led by Sultan Khalil surrounded the double fortifications of the city of Acre. Two hundred years after the first Crusader army had conquered Jerusalem, the town that they had named St. John's Acre was all that remained of the Christian presence that was supposed to have been established in Palestine. The Muslim army was convinced that the Christians could be driven into the sea if Acre fell, so their attack was fierce. The Christian defense was led in the north by the Knights Templar, while the Teutons and the Knights of St. John were responsible for defending the southern wall. French and English knights sustained the eastern line, and merchants from Venice and Pisa, which had become economically powerful as a result of the Crusades, guarded the western wall.

The onslaught was violent, but the defending warriors, who had no option but to fight until the end, put up tremendous resistance. Such a heated battle was a fitting conclusion to the Crusaders' grand campaign.

According to the Arab chroniclers, "The Muslim army killed many of the city's residents, pillaged extensively, and took as prisoners all those they did not kill. Then, after beheading the last of the city dwellers in front of the ramparts, they razed the city." So many Christians were sold into slavery it was said a young girl couldn't even fetch a single piece of silver. According to an Arab account, "All of Palestine was once again returned to Muslim hands, and the coastline was cleansed of Franks all the way from Syria down to Egypt. Praise be to Allah!"

Those from the Italian seaside city-states who could return to their homelands were the fortunate ones. Two hundred years is a long time, however. For those born and raised in Palestine, no home remained to which they could return. Their retreat must have been miserable as they clung to any boat in sight and weathered the rough seas. The knights left behind were nearly annihilated, and of the few who survived the battle, even fewer survived the 300-kilometer exodus to Cyprus. The seriously wounded Grand Master of the Knights Templar and Jean de Villiers, Grand Master of the Knights of St. John, who was also gravely injured, were among those fortunate enough to escape. Cyprus, which Richard the Lionhearted had conquered a hundred years earlier almost as an afterthought, became the refuge for the Christians who had been driven into the Mediterranean, if only for the moment.

When Richard I of England, who had taken no interest in long-term prospects, conquered the island practically on a whim, its control shifted from the Byzantine Empire to the Christians of Western Europe. The king handed the island's administration over to the Knights Templar, but their rule was unsuccessful. Perhaps they were too preoccupied with their mighty stronghold in Palestine to trouble themselves with the management of Cyprus. That may also be the reason that they sold the island for 100,000 ducats to Guy of Lusignan, a minor French nobleman who had traveled to Palestine. Cyprus remained in his family's control until 1474.

The Knights Templar must have regretted their rash decision to sell Cyrpus when they were granted permission, along with others, to stay on the island as refugees by Lusignan's descendant Henry II. While refugees may gain sympathy, they are never truly welcomed. The Cypriot king, afraid that the knights would wrest control of the island from him, didn't permit any of the refugees to own land. These circumstances brought the knightly orders face to face with the most serious crisis in their history.

A Time of Trials

The three main religious knightly orders of St. John, Templar, and Teuton, as well as various smaller groups created during the medieval period, shared essentially the same objectives:

To preserve for Christian believers the Holy Sepulcher that is Christ's tomb, as well as Jerusalem, the Holy Land that surrounds the tomb, and to protect same from the attacks of non-believers until the resurrection of Christ.

To guarantee the safety of Christians living in the region and pilgrims who come to visit the Holy Land.

To care for the sick and those wounded in defense of the Holy Land.

To search for Christians sold into slavery after falling into enemy hands and to secure their freedom.

But the knights became unable to achieve any of these objectives during their stay on Cyprus. They still attempted to free Christian slaves, but as they were refugees with little funds, and particularly since the Muslims with whom they were dealing only cared about fetching the highest prices, they had little success. They sent numerous delegations to Europe to advocate the formation of another Crusader army that would use Cyprus as a foothold to launch a campaign to recapture the Holy Land, but the European rulers, who had entrusted the defense of the Holy Land to the knights for more than half a century, were now concentrating on expanding their influence within Europe. Noncommittal replies came back one after another. The Western powers were no longer interested in Palestine. The refugees on Cyprus had no choice but to accept their isolation.

Having lost their reason for existence, the knightly orders' dissolution seemed virtually inevitable. All that remained for them was either to discover a way to regain their original justification or to adapt to their circumstances and find a new role. After returning to Europe, the smaller orders simply disappeared as if they had just died out. The Teutonic Knights also returned to Europe and devoted themselves to the colonization of Prussia. The worst fate was reserved for the Knights Templar.

The French king, who was moving aggressively to strengthen his monarchy, noticed the Knights Templar's great wealth and vast land holdings. Determined to take their money and estates for himself, the king set out to annihilate them. Crimes such as heresy and conspiracy were given as the justification. Modern historians cannot confirm whether the king's accusations were based in fact, but the Knights' high-interest money lending and their dealings with Muslims were likely invoked to fabricate the pretexts used to destroy them. One after another, the knights were tortured or burned alive, and when their Grand Master was put to death in 1314, the order came to an end.

There are no reliable historical sources to tell us exactly why the Knights of St. John, who had amassed a fortune of their own, managed to escape the same fate. Some believe they benefited from the famous lack of policy of Pope Clement V, who had played a part in the destruction of the Templars. The fact that the Knights of

St. John were more adaptable than the Knights Templar, however, surely contributed to this outcome.

Forced to live like refugees on Cyprus, the Knights of St. John soon exchanged the horses they had been riding in Palestine for boats. They became pirates, although they only targeted Muslims. They also devoted their efforts to running hospitals, the mission they had pursued since the order's establishment. The rulers of Western Europe, who already had misgivings about the destruction of the Knights Templar, now found themselves incapable of raising a finger against the Knights of St. John.

Yet regardless of whether they found success as pirates or dedicated themselves to healing the sick, as long as the Knights of St. John remained on Cyprus they would be nothing more than lodgers subject to the whims of the king. They were an order, after all, that had controlled numerous independent estates in Palestine, including the Krak des Chevalier, a fortress praised in its day as the sturdiest and most magnificent on earth and is the largest Crusader stronghold that still stands today. They knew better than anyone the importance of maintaining an independent base, and that became their primary goal.

The opportunity to realize this ambition arrived, completely unexpectedly, fifteen years after the Knights of St. John escaped to Cyprus, when a Genoese pirate named Vignoli came to ask for their cooperation in a certain undertaking.

Bound for Rhodes

Vignoli had somehow managed to rent the islands of Kos and Leros from the Byzantine Emperor, whose empire was in decline. He planned to add Rhodes to his holdings and conquer all the islands in that part of the sea. As he didn't have enough military strength to do so without aid, he decided to try to convince the Knights of St. John, who were enjoying success in the same "profession," to contribute their boats and troops and fight alongside him. His only condition was that they pay him a third of the annual revenues from the lands they succeeded in subjugating. Foulques de Villaret, the Grand Master at the time, jumped at the offer.

The Knights first attacked Rhodes in 1306, but were turned back by the fierce resistance of the troops garrisoned on the island, subjects of the Byzantine Empire to which the island rightfully belonged. The Knights, however, were committed to securing a stronghold of their own and didn't lose morale easily. After several campaigns, they finally conquered the island in 1308. The Byzantine Empire protested, but the protests of a polity without the military strength to take the island back were nothing more than words. The Europeans, on the other hand, were thrilled to have a new base for the Crusaders. The pope even issued a decree recognizing the order's ownership of the island.

It is unclear whether the Knights, who once again had their own fortress, actually kept their promise to pay the Genoese pirates a third of the revenue they acquired from Rhodes. Judging from the history of these "warriors for Christ," it seems probable that the Knights deceived the pirates brilliantly. On the other hand, they were determined to return in full the money they had borrowed from Venetian banks to finance their campaign to seize Rhodes, though it would take them twenty years to settle the loans. This disparity may have been due to the fact that the Knights had a greater affinity for Venice than for Genoa, which were the two major rival powers in the Mediterranean. Unlike Genoa, which tended to avoid interfering in the affairs of its individual citizens, the Republic of Venice believed that something deemed bad for one was bad for all. Now that they had their own base, the Knights could not afford to make the mistake of turning the Venetians, who represented the strongest presence in the Mediterranean, into enemies.

In 1310, the Knights of St. John completed their relocation from their borrowed home on Cyprus to Rhodes, where they were masters of their own domain. That year marked the beginning of a second era for the Knights. This was also when people started referring to them as the Knights of Rhodes. Even the Byzantine Emperor had no choice but to acknowledge their unquestionable control of the island. All of this happened while the fires consuming the bodies of the Knights Templar in France were burning at their brightest.

Chapter Three

The Lair of

Christian Vipers

Ancient Rhodes

The Isle of Rhodes floats in the southeast of the Aegean Sea like a rugby ball tilted from southwest to northeast, so close to Asia Minor that it looks like it might be swallowed up at any moment. The total area of the island is less than 1500 square kilometers. It is no longer than 80 kilometers and no wider than 38 kilometers at any point. A mountain range runs the length of the island like a spine, but there is only one tall mountain, measuring 1200 meters. Arable land is not abundant.

The island's ideal climate has made it famous since ancient times. The temperature in the towns never drops below 50 degrees Fahrenheit, even during the coldest month of February, and it rarely rises above 77 degrees in the shade during the hottest month of August. If the temperature were to reach 86 degrees, even in direct sunlight, that would be considered a truly remarkable summer. Even though the rainy season lasts from November to April, there are never any continuous, gloomy downpours. Rather, strong rains come suddenly and then quickly subside.

While the winds of the Mediterranean are characterized by their constant changes in direction, the seas around Rhodes are visited by uniform seasonal winds. The Mistral blows from spring to summer out of the northwest, and the two winds that blow between autumn and winter are the southeast wind called the Scirocco and the southwest wind called the Libeccio. Since cool winds blow during the hot season and the winds turn warm when the air grows cold, the island's reputation for having a *dolce*, or "sweet," climate is warranted. Thanks to the numerous streams that flow down from the mountains, water has always been plentiful. If the verdant isle ever lacked anything, it was wheat. But this scarcity was only felt if the need was great.

The good harbors are all gathered along the north-eastern shore. Among these, the port of Rhodes at the northernmost tip of the island, and Lindos in the middle of the eastern side of the island, have been considered the key harbors since antiquity. Through the ages, Rhodes has always been the capital city.

It was inevitable that people would notice this paradise in the Mediterranean. At the very beginning of written history, around 1500 BC, emigrants from Crete began to settle the northern part of the island. Much like the islands of the Aegean Sea, Rhodes has shared in the vicissitudes of the Greek people.

From about 800 BC, the island's optimal location allowed it to prosper as an important trading outpost, helping it join the ranks of Ionian cities along the nearby west coast of Asia Minor such as Ephesus, Miletus, and Halicarnassus. Emigrants from Rhodes also built many colonies along the Mediterranean coast.

But unlike the Ionian cities, which were on the Asian continent, the island's location at sea allowed it to avoid falling under Persian control when the Persians attacked in the fifth century BC. Rhodes contributed its warships to the anti-Persian Delian League led by Athens. Even when Greece was split into Spartan and Athenian factions and Rhodes was forced to associate with both sides in turn, it was able to maintain a satisfactory degree of independence. But with the rise of Alexander the Great, perhaps because his strength was so overwhelming, Rhodes took the initiative and joined forces with Macedonia.

It is probably safe to say that the brightest era in the history of Rhodes started after Alexander's death. The island's close trading relations with Egypt brought a level of prosperity rivaling that of Alexandria in Egypt and Syracuse in Sicily. A giant statue that straddled the port, known as the Colossus of Rhodes, was built during this period. One of the Seven Wonders of the Ancient World, this massive bronze statue was toppled by the terrible earthquake of 227 BC, but there is no doubt that Rhodes possessed the highest level of technology known to man at the time. The Seven Wonders, which include the pyramids of Egypt, were, after all, such awe-inspiring structures that no one could believe they had been built by human hands.

The people of Rhodes excelled in the arts as well as technology. The Winged Victory of Samothrace, now on display at the Louvre, is believed to have been the creation of a Rhodian in the second century BC, and the Vatican Museum's Laocoön Group is thought to be a Roman copy of a Rhodian sculpture. The number of works extant in the art museum on Rhodes bearing the mark of Ancient Greece gives one a sense of just how many of its works must have scattered across the earth over the course of two thousand years.

The fame of Rhodes had begun to fade towards the beginning of the Common Era, when Julius Caesar and other sons of ancient Roman nobility visited the island for their education. Having been Roman territory, Rhodes was added to the eastern Byzantine Empire in 395 AD when the Roman Empire was split into eastern and western halves. Rhodes fell into obscurity for quite some time after this, but resurfaced in the tenth century when Italian merchant ships began to move through the region. Rhodes would sometimes fall under the direct control of the Byzantines, sometimes align with the Venetians, and occasionally be forced to open its harbors to the Genoese. Overall, the tiny island's fortunes were inextricably tied with those of the Byzantine Empire.

Then in 1310, the Knights of St. John conquered the island. While the people of Rhodes had once been the bearers of a higher civilization, they were now in no position to call the Frenchmen of the order "barbarians," even if the French at the time had no advanced civilization of their own.

The Coming of the Knights

The Greek natives scattered around Rhodes numbered around fifty thousand. It may seem hard to believe that no Greeks ever revolted against the occupation by the Knights of St. John, a group accounting for only one hundredth of the island's total population, and who furthermore adhered to different customs and beliefs. The Greeks' inaction was due to many factors not limited to the loss of their former glory.

With the rise of centralized states in the late fifteenth century, rule based on the principle of quantity would replace rule based on the principle of quality. The order was fortunately still able to maintain long-term rule on the basis of quality. Seafarers such as the Venetians and the Genoese were not the only ones who succeeded in using small groups of people to operate trading and military outposts in distant lands where it would be costly and time-consuming to dispatch reinforcement troops. The kingdom of Cyprus did the same, and until they were driven out of Palestine, so did the Crusaders. The Knights of St. John had a stronghold on Rhodes and had only to consider how best to put their "quality" to use.

To begin with, the Greek natives of Rhodes hadn't become subject to a ruling class whose only thought was how to exploit them. The Knights had abundant wealth. Once the profits from their investments in Europe started to flow in reliably, there was no need for them to depend on revenue from the Rhodians. Not only that, but their resources in Europe were constantly increasing. Now that the Teutonic Knights had scattered to the coast of the Baltic Sea and the Knights Templar had been destroyed, the Knights of St. John were the only remaining order able to combat the infidels with that special combination of chivalry and monkish devotion. It was only natural that donations and transfers of inheritance began to flow from the faithful into their coffers. They were the only ones still waging guerrilla warfare against Muslims in the Orient; it didn't bother most Europeans at the time that the Knights were hardly different from pirates.

Insofar as they had to endure occupation, the Rhodians were fortunate to have found congenial rulers in the Knights: they were fellow Christians, at least, and they were rich. Moreover, the Knights absolutely relied on their subjects in order to continue executing their essential mission.

A number of islands dotted the seas surrounding Rhodes. Now that the Knights of St. John had the main island firmly in their grasp, they gradually began placing all of these other islands within their sphere of influence, starting with the tiny outcroppings nearby and extending to the comparatively large isles of Kos and Leros. They even managed to gain control of Halicarnassus (already called Bodrum by that time), a port town at the southwestern tip of Asia Minor. They also occupied the key town of Smyrna in Asia Minor until it was taken by Timur. Since the Knights planned to use Rhodes as a base from which to attack Muslim ships in the region, these were all absolutely necessary conquests.

They built lookout fortresses on the islands, while the islands themselves, then still rich with greenery, provided the lumber they needed to build ships. The Knights consolidated their sphere of influence in less than half a century. Conveniently for them, and inconveniently for their Muslim enemies, Rhodes occupied the seam tying together the rising Islamic power of Turkey and the long-standing Islamic power of Egypt. Ironically, the Knights' presence in the Eastern Mediterranean grew for the next hundred and fifty years directly in proportion to the spread of Turkish rule in the region.

The fall of the Byzantine Empire in 1453 and the conquests of Syria and Egypt in 1517 ensured the continuation of this trend. These two pivotal Turkish victories turned the Eastern Mediterranean into the inland sea of the Ottoman Empire, and precisely for that reason the presence of heretics within the waters became troublesome. Known as the "bone stuck in the throat of Islam" during their years in Palestine, the Knights came to be called the "Christian vipers" after their move to Rhodes. For the Muslims, the Isle of Rhodes was a snake pit.

These "vipers," or knights-turned-pirates, learned traditional nautical skills from the Greek natives of Rhodes. Although peerless in battle, the aristocratic knights were not confident seafarers. It was considered unseemly for them, as nobles, to meddle with boats, which were redolent of merchants and commerce. It was thought that those with "blue blood" should devote themselves to battle, man's highest calling.

Thus the interests of the rulers and the ruled on Rhodes and the surrounding islands came into a curious alignment. European merchant ships became a common sight in the ports of Rhodes now that Western Europeans had taken over the island. There were many Genoese ships, and not a few merchants from Provence and Catalonia also settled on the island. The Jewish quarters were also a center of trade. It seemed that Rhodes was slowly recovering after having languished since the collapse of the ancient world.

Rebuilding the Nest

The Order of the Knights of St. John had controlled the Krak des Chevaliers, the mightiest fortress in Palestine. While the capital city of Rhodes had a proud tradition of affluence reaching back to antiquity, the durability of the stronghold the Knights began constructing there was unlike anything the island had ever seen. After being divided into merchant and military sections, the ports were expanded and fully fortified. Like the castle walls, the ports had to be continually modified to adapt to advances in weaponry and changes in tactics, so there was no end to the Knights' planning. Now that Palestine was lost, Rhodes was on the front line of the battle against Islam. The Knights had to be in a perpetual state of readiness.

Keeping the entire island on a constant war footing necessitated restructuring the order in an appropriately military fashion. The Knights had already militarized considerably during the age of the Crusades and had gone even further in that direction after relocating to Rhodes. The order itself was broken up into independent units according to the knights' native languages. Italy, England, and Germany each constituted a linguistic group. There were many scions of aristocratic families from southern German lands in the German corps; the Teutonic Knights, although hidden away in Prussia, were still in existence. The Spanish began as one unit, but soon split into two: one consisting mainly of Spaniards from the Castilian region as well as some Portuguese, and the other comprising Spaniards from Aragon as well as Navarre and Catalonia. The former came to be called the Castilian unit, and the latter the Spanish or Aragonese unit.

From the time of the Crusades, the French had always provided the largest number of knights. This was still true when they moved to Rhodes, where the French were split into three units: one from Ile-de-France (simply called the French unit), one from Provence, and one from Auvergne. Numerical balance was not always maintained among the various units, and even after they were divided, the three French and the two Spanish units enjoyed a consistent superiority in numbers. Each unit had its own residence, which functioned as a kind of headquarters. The residences of the French and Spanish units were also grander than the rest.

Each of the eight units had a commander. These men, along with the Grand Master, the Lieutenant Grand

Master, and the Archbishop of Rhodes, comprised the General Staff Office, which was the supreme decision-making body of the Order of the Knights of St. John. Since this committee held the power to dismiss any of the knights, it was the order's legislative, executive, and judicial branches combined into one. The committee was also entrusted with overseeing the Knights' European investments and governing the populations of Rhodes and the surrounding islands.

Knights who belonged to the residences were ranked below the members of the committee. The superintendents of the order's fortresses in various regions, as well as the captains of their fighting vessels, were all selected from among this officer class. When knights reached old age and retired, it became their job to invest the monies that the order held in Europe. But since they were almost constantly at war, many of those on Rhodes died in battle and never made it back home. Since the order replenished its numbers often, with newcomers from Europe, the average age of a knight stationed in the Orient was always quite young.

The above were of noble blood. They were members of a religious order who, like monks, had taken the three cardinal vows of poverty, obedience, and chastity. They were of course not allowed to marry. Their numbers in the Orient, for which Rhodes was the main base, never rose above five or six hundred even in the face of an anticipated enemy assault.

Some knights remained in Europe without once setting foot on Rhodes, but these were mostly the scions of the most powerful royal and aristocratic families. In many cases, they held the highest positions, such as cardinal, within the Roman Catholic Church. A member of the Medici family and brother-in-law of Pope Leo X, Cardinal Giulio de'Medici, who eventually became Pope Clement VII, was one of the Knights of St. John who had never seen battle against the Muslims.

Below the officers were the valets, native Rhodian sailors, and doctors who worked in the hospitals, all of whom were the equivalent of noncommissioned officers. These men obviously didn't need to be of noble descent, nor did they need to take monastic vows. The knights were required to serve in the hospitals once a week, but in those days few noblemen aspired to learn the art of medicine. Thus, even within a Catholic order such as the Knights Hospitaller, most of the full-time doctors were Jews.

Latin was the official language of the order, and also the universal language of the time, but both French and Italian were spoken in meetings. French was obviously used because there were so many French knights. Italian, on the other hand, was used because so many of the engineers responsible for the critical job of building and repairing the fortresses, as well as the merchants in charge of provisions and transportation, were Italian. The knights of course spoke their respective native languages within the residences.

The Hospital

As the sobriquet "Hospitallers" suggests, caring for the sick was one of the order's most important activities. The hospital the Knights built on Rhodes was second in grandeur only to the Grand Master's Palace. Traditionally, the head of the hospital was the commander of one of the three French units, Ile-de-France, Provence, and Auvergne. Incidentally, the English commander served as head of the cavalry, while the Italian commander acted as chief of the navy.

The initial objective of the Amalfian merchants who had built the first hospitals in Palestine had been to care for pilgrims who fell ill in the Holy Land. With the beginning of the Crusades came the additional objective of healing warriors wounded in battle against infidels in protection of the Holy Land. These objectives were upheld after the move to Rhodes, albeit with significant adjustments.

At the end of the thirteenth century, when European Christians lost their last foothold in Palestine, pilgrimages to the Holy Land came to a momentary halt. Before long, however, various European countries (beginning with Venice) started to plan group pilgrimages to the Holy Land. Although the Muslims had achieved their goal of driving the Christians back into the Mediterranean, they couldn't afford to spurn the money that Western pilgrims brought into the region. A compromise was reached. As Rhodes was close to the Holy Land, it became a convenient place for pilgrim ships traveling between Europe and Palestine to drop off sick pilgrims.

Cyprus was annexed by the Republic of Venice in 1489, and from then on Western ships always called on that port. But for 150 years, the hospital on Rhodes was the one facility where ailing Europeans far from home could expect to be as safe as possible while receiving the finest care available. Since the patients included princes and other people of importance in addition to common pilgrims, working to improve the quality of care and comfort at the hospital was an investment that returned high dividends for the order. The Muslims controlling Jerusalem had allowed Christians to build monasteries within the city, but these were used only for lodgings and were not at all satisfactory when it came to caring for the sick.

Although their second objective of tending to warriors wounded while protecting the Holy Land was nearly moot, the Knights did carry on the role of protecting Christians from the violence of non-believers.

The order attacked any ship that appeared to belong to Muslims. They did this not only to kill or imprison the crew, sink or commandeer the ships, or steal all of the cargo; since Turkish ships commonly used Christian slaves as oarsmen, the Knights were also fighting for the just cause of freeing these men from their chains. As the Knights Hospitaller saw it, these were warriors who had fallen in the righteous struggle to protect Christians from heathens. Needless to say, the order's own knights were also entitled to receive comprehensive medical attention.

For all of these reasons, the Knights' hospital on Rhodes was not only a magnificent building to behold but also a place that provided the finest care possible at the time. It was said, in fact, that only the hospitals in Venice were its equal. The full-time medical staff consisted of two physicians, four surgeons, and the knights, who were required to serve once a week in the hospital as nurses. Single beds were arranged in a spacious room with a high ceiling. Up to a hundred people could be accommodated in this common room, and each bed had a curtain that could be drawn around it. Patients did not have to pile up personal effects or luggage around or under their beds. Such things could be stored in the small closets along the room's walls. There was also a cafeteria for the patients who could walk, and mass was given every morning in the small chapel in the middle of the room. There were also seven private rooms.

Patients were not charged for their medical expenses regardless of their wealth, not even for use of a private room. Meals were the same for everyone, and these were also free. The hospital served what was, at the time, a rather extravagant fare of white bread, wine, meat, and boiled vegetables. They also used hemp sheets and silver utensils decorated with the crests of the most illustrious families of Europe, items bequeathed to them by knights who had died. There was even a garden right off of the rooms on the ground floor that, although not large, permitted strolls under the shade of the lush southern greenery. It was no wonder that the hospital flourished and that it frequently had to renovate and expand.

Gambling was prohibited within the hospital. It was also forbidden to speak in a loud voice. Patients could have visitors, but there were never so many visitors that the knights had to worry about their disturbing the other patients. Few families could come running to see pilgrims who had fallen ill on an island in the distant Orient, and knights recovering from battlefield injuries were all also separated from their families.

"The Christian Vipers"

Hospital administration, for which the Knights were known, thus continued to progress smoothly as did their other affair, piracy. Since the retreat of the Western powers from the Eastern Mediterranean and the rise of the Turks, the seas around Rhodes increasingly became a primary sea-lane. Ships headed for Egypt or Syria setting off from the main Turkish ports of Constantinople or Gallipoli simply had to pass Rhodes. It was the natural choice in terms of distance and for nautical reasons. The Turks were neither traders nor accomplished seafarers so they always tried to stay as close to shore as possible. They often relied on Greek sailors under their rule, but even the Greeks were only accustomed to the Aegean, where one could always make out the shapes of islands in the distance. They were no match for Venetian or Genoese sailors who calmly undertook voyages across open seas. Thus, Turkish ships traveled as far south as possible along the Turkish-controlled coast after leaving port, after which they had no choice but to sail out of the Aegean and into the Mediterranean. Rhodes was located precisely at the border of the two seas, which allowed the knightly pirates to keep rather busy.

The seas around Rhodes, unusually for the Mediterranean, experienced winds that blew in one fixed direction throughout each season. As a result, the air remained clear, with ideal visibility, for long stretches at a time. The waters were not very deep since they were a direct extension of the waters of the Aegean; waves thus rose with the slightest wind. There was also a northward current that flowed at a speed of 0.5 to 2 knots. While these were not particularly adverse conditions for the Turkish ships, they were always—with the exception of genuine pirate vessels—manned by inferior sailors. Meanwhile, the pilots of the Knights' ships were Rhodian natives who had known these waters since childhood.

Until the Battle of Trafalgar, when ships began attacking each other with cannons, "sea battles" simply meant pulling close to an enemy ship, boarding it, and engaging the opponent in close combat. As long as you could get close to the enemy ship, these battles were really no different from battles on land, and the "blue-blooded" Knights of St. John excelled at such melees. The combination of their fierce bravery and the skillful sailing of the Rhodians put terror into the hearts of the Turks. Of course, nothing makes a warrior stronger than a constant state of preparedness, and in this, too, the Knights achieved an ideal standard.

The naval power of the Knights still didn't compare with that of the Venetians, either in quality or in quantity. Nor could they approach the Turks or the Spaniards in terms of sheer quantity. There was no need for the Knights, however, to cover a wide battlefield. As long as they patrolled the seas around their island their prey naturally came to them. They used their territory to great advantage by building their fortresses and bases in the most strategic locations. Unlike ships that had to travel greater distances, the Knights' vessels could return home after a single day's voyage and thus did not have to carry unnecessary cargo. Instead, they could simply crowd their ships with all the troops they would need in battle. Though only half the size of the large three-mast Venetian galleys, the Knights' ships had the same number of masts. Their fast galleys, built specifically for battles in the waters off Rhodes, were the linch-pin of their navy. They could easily reach cruising speeds of 4.5 to 7 knots.

The Knights' ships differed in another way from those of the Venetians and the Genoese. Unlike the sea-faring Italians, who used their own citizens as oarsmen so that they could join the melee once an enemy ship had

been boarded, the Knights primarily used Muslim prisoners as slaves to row their ships. As a result, they couldn't
let their oarsmen sit on the main deck as the Italians did.
Bound by wooden chains, the oarsmen rowed just below
the deck in a low-ceilinged compartment. The last thing
the Knights wanted when engaging Muslims in open
combat was to have their own Muslim oarsmen sneaking
up behind them. This practice of using heathen slaves as
oarsmen, of course, was shared by the Turks, who used
Christians.

Whenever a signal fire was lit on one of their
fortresses, the knights on Rhodes launched a fleet of four
ships. Each ship usually carried a crew of one hundred
oarsmen, twenty sailors, and fifty knights. First, two of
the ships would sail toward the approaching enemy vessel,
overshoot it, and turn around to attack it from behind.
The two remaining ships would confront their prey head
on. Once they had the enemy ship pinned like this, they
would draw in as close as possible. When they were close
enough that their oars were touching, they would throw
"Greek fire" on board the enemy vessel.

The Turkish ships, of course, didn't casually sail
into these dangerous waters one by one. They usually
sailed in convoys of four or five, and sometimes even in
fleets of ten. The Knights, based upon information from
their lookouts, adjusted the size of their attack force
accordingly. There were times when two ships would
square off against a single enemy; at other times, ships

would battle one on one. Even then, the superior sailing and fighting of the Christian crews were more than enough to terrorize the Turks. To them the white cross on red atop the Knights' masts announced the arrival of the devil.

The incendiary weapon commonly called "Greek fire" is said to have been invented by a man from Byzantium, and the Crusaders, too, used it during their time in Palestine. It was a mixture of potassium nitrate, sulfur, ammonium salt, and resin, but the proportions of the mixture were kept secret and are now lost.

The substance had many different uses. Sometimes it was pushed into a long brass pipe, set on fire, and pointed at the enemy like a modern flamethrower. There was also a device similar to a grenade, made from round terracotta flasks, that could be thrown aboard enemy ships. Using the same type of flask, one could make a bomb by inserting a fuse and lighting it. The Byzantines apparently developed a way to have the fire billow out of the mouths of the wooden animals decorating the bows of their boats, but the Knights of St. John didn't borrow this method. They were probably afraid their own ships would go up in flames.

Whatever the technique, once this "Greek fire" was thrown aboard an enemy ship, which in those days would have been made almost entirely of wood, everything from the deck to the masts to the sails was immediately enveloped in flames. Having thus thrown the enemy into disarray, the knights in their steel armor charged in. They may no longer have had steeds, but the tactic eminently suited the martial spirit of the medievalist knights.

The Order of St. John never had a large fleet, but by doggedly pursuing guerrilla warfare with what they had, they profited immensely. Enemy boats were burned, the crews were either killed or taken prisoner, and huge ransoms were collected in exchange for hostages. Since the Knights also stole cargo, Turkish ships that wanted to avoid being plundered had no choice but to rely on the protection of a great fleet. Yet, the Ottoman Empire, never a naval power, didn't have the resources to send a convoy with each ship that made its way along this heavily trafficked sea-lane. The Knights were able to legitimize their piracy by claiming they were attacking infidels and liberating Christian slaves from their chains.

There were times when the Knights were so single-minded in their hatred for Muslims that relations soured even with their fellow Christians. This was especially true of their dealings with the Republic of Venice, which, as a trading state, embraced a more pragmatic outlook.

One year a Venetian ship sailing along the North African coast was attacked by one of the order's ships, which frequently went out on expeditions. Not only was the Venetian ship towed back to Rhodes, but ten Arab passengers aboard the ship were sold as slaves. This took place before the collapse of the Byzantine Empire that resulted from the fall of Constantinople in 1453; at that time the Venetians and the Turks were not yet in conflict.

When the Venetian government heard the news, they immediately dispatched their fleet stationed on Crete; they considered it their duty to ensure the safety of the passengers on their ships, regardless of faith. The Venetians blocked the entrance to the port of Rhodes with their galleys and trained their guns directly on the port's walls, pressing hard for the Knights either to return the Arabs or to engage in battle. The Knights returned the Venetian ship, along with all of its passengers.

In the latter half of the fifteenth century, the Republic of Venice fought two wars, albeit reluctantly, against the Turks. During the peaceful interludes between these battles, the Order of the Knights of St. John openly attacked Venetian merchant ships. As they saw it, Christians who made treaties with the infidels were more hateful than the infidels themselves. It was this very single-mindedness that had allowed them to justify their existence as a religious order of knights even after they had lost Palestine. The attitude became ingrained not only for spiritual reasons, but because it invited charitable donations of land and money. The Knights were charting the only course left to them.

Unlike the Republic of Venice, the Order of the Knights of St. John did not need to make a living by trade. Indeed, they survived precisely by shunning commerce. With the decline of Genoa, the Knights and the Venetians became the two forces resisting the Turks in the Eastern Mediterranean and their relationship grew more complicated.

No member of Venice's powerful aristocratic households ever entered the Order of the Knights of St. John. This was partly because the Knights didn't acknowledge the nobility of "nobles" who relied on trade, even if the order included members of the Medici household, who were urban aristocrats, as well as a number of Genoese. But the main reason there were no Venetians in the order was that the Venetian government didn't allow it.

Be that as it may, for a state that made its living as Venice did, nothing could be more foolish or self-defeating than antagonizing a powerful entity. Venice met the demands of the Order of the Knights of St. John openly when the situation allowed it, and secretly when it didn't. The Knights hardly seemed to notice when their demands were being met only behind the scenes. Apparently, the idea of deceiving your allies in order to deceive your enemies was not something that ran in the "blue blood" of the medieval warriors.

Mehmed II, The Conqueror

The rising Turkish nation, whose influence was widening by the day, didn't simply sit back with arms folded and leave the knights on Rhodes to themselves. After successfully destroying the Byzantine Empire in 1453, Sultan Mehmed II sought hegemony in the Mediterranean world with such fervor that he moved his capital to Constantinople and declared himself the successor of the Byzantines. In 1480, he sent an army of 100,000 troops to conquer Rhodes. The Order of the Knights of St. John, under the command of Grand Master Pierre d'Aubusson, withstood the three-month siege. The defending army, which numbered no more than six hundred if one only counted the knights, withstood the invasion thanks in part to an epidemic among the Turkish troops; moreover, the sultan's absence had resulted in an inconsistent strategy on the part of his generals.

This defeat, which for the Turks was neither a major disgrace nor a setback to their morale, became for the Knights of St. John a victory of such great importance that one had to go back three centuries, to their time in Palestine, to find its equal. They had succeeded in facing down and driving back the Turks, whom neither the Byzantine Empire nor Venice, queen of the sea, had been able to defeat. For Christendom, it was a brilliant accomplishment. The countries of Western Europe celebrated it as if they had finally become aware again of the Knights' existence. D'Aubusson was bestowed the rank of cardinal, something that had never happened to any other Grand Master in the history of the order. It goes without saying that donations and the number of volunteers increased dramatically.

Never for a minute, though, did the Knights think that the Turks would just leave it at that. For the next forty years, they devoted themselves to strengthening the order's defenses. The Italian Fabrizio del Carretto, Grand

Master between 1513 and 1522, deserves particular mention for transforming the design of the walls to fortify them against cannons, the most important weapons of warfare after the fall of Constantinople. As a native of Italy, one of the most technologically advanced lands in those days, he understood that the age when victory was decided by valor alone had come to an end.

The only reason the order was able to spend those forty years in relative tranquility was that the Turks were not seriously interested in Rhodes during that time. Mehmed II's son Beyazid had to consolidate the great empire that his father had gained haphazardly. Under Mehmed's grandson Selim, the Turks succeeded in capturing Syria, Arabia, and Egypt, all lands they had long coveted. These conquests were completed in 1517 and allowed the Turks—who had taken control of Mecca— to become the spiritual leader of Islam. The Eastern Mediterranean was their own inland sea, and now the time had come to attend to that thorn, the Isle of Rhodes.

Cyprus and Crete were the other two Christian fortresses floating within this "inland sea." Both were held by the Republic of Venice, then still a formidable naval power. Rhodes, in contrast, seemed to the Turks to be an island guarded by no more than a handful of men. In contrast to the Venetian islands, whose people were certainly not pirates, the Turks could justify conquering Rhodes as a rooting out of pillagers. Their opponents would be armed monks, cross held high at the front of their ranks. Such a cause was completely acceptable within the context of Islamic justice. It was Suleiman, who ascended to the sultan's throne in 1520, who finally made the decision to subjugate Rhodes.

With a confrontation looming with the House of Hapsburg, then the rising power in the West, the young sultan must have realized that his empire could no longer suffer the Knights and the "nest of Christian vipers" to remain on the Isel of Rhodes. Suleiman had successfully conquered Belgrade on an expedition to Hungary a year after taking the throne. He was now ready to set his sights on Rhodes.

Sultan Suleiman I

Sultan Mehmed II was not the "founder" of the Ottoman Empire if we define the word to mean fashioning something out of nothing. Yet we can certainly think of him as such in that he destroyed the Byzantine Empire and gave the Turkish people a course to follow. The reign of Sultan Suleiman, who came to be revered as "Suleiman the Magnificent," followed those of Beyazid and Selim, so he was not, strictly speaking, the third generation. But in every other sense, Suleiman was the proverbial third.

Upon assuming the throne at the age of nineteen, his great-grandfather Mehmed II had established the precedent of killing one's brothers to forestall a struggle for the throne. His grandfather Beyazid had neglected to follow this practice, and as a result one of his younger brothers, Cem (pronounced like the English word "gem"), rebelled against him. While he was able to suppress the rebellion, he also had to endure the bitter experience of seeing Cem escape to Rhodes.

The Grand Master of the Order of the Knights of St. John felt that keeping such a precious hostage, who had come tumbling into Rhodes from afar, would give the Turks justification for an attack. He therefore sent Cem to the king of his own France. Pope Alexander VI (Rodrigo Borgia) then took custody of him, thinking he might serve as a shield against Turkish attack. The prince therefore came to lead an elegant life as a hostage in Rome. It goes without saying that his brother Beyazid in Constantinople wished for a more complete banishment. The sultan sent a letter to the pope to the following effect:

> The Sultan of the Ottoman Empire, whose thoughts are filled with the sad plight of his hostage brother, and who believes that freeing him from endless days of misery is the proper desire of his own flesh and blood, has in due course reached a decision. Freeing Cem from the suffering of this world and sending him to the next would surely allow his spirit to attain a greater peace. We are prepared to offer 300,000 ducats to Your Holiness as a token of our gratitude in exchange for said dispensation of kindness.

Nearly equal to the entire fortune of the Medici family, this vast reward must have been quite enticing for Borgia, who was famous for being free with his money. Yet he was also an unusually political man who knew that hostages became more valuable the longer one kept them alive. The Turkish prince-in-exile thus managed to avoid a lethal serving of "Borgia's poison." Several years later, however, he was forced to accompany the King of France, who had invaded Italy; en route to Naples he contracted malaria and died.

Perhaps wishing to avoid a repeat of such a scandal, upon taking the throne, Selim, the next sultan, immediately had his two younger brothers killed, along with their wives, mistresses, and children—seventeen kin in all. Though Selim had a number of daughters, Suleiman was his only son. Suleiman therefore eluded having to occupy a throne drenched in blood.

In what may be a reflection of these circumstances, Suleiman wanted, from the very moment he took the throne at twenty-five, to be known as a "man of law" and a "disciplined ruler." He relished demonstrating such qualities whenever the opportunity presented itself. He may have been determined to conquer Rhodes, but sending an army unannounced was not part of his plan. In 1521, he sent a personal letter to Philippe Villiers de L'Isle-Adam, who had just succeeded Fabrizio del Carretto as the Grand Master of the Knights.

Suleiman was certainly better educated than, say,

Charles of the House of Hapsburg, and the letter, written in superb Latin, came from his own pen. It listed the Turkish forces' victories of that year, and told of how they had conquered beautiful cities that had been amply fortified against attack—of how they'd killed many residents and turned survivors into slaves. The letter concluded by asking the Grand Master of the Order of the Knights of St. John, who had lived for so many years as his neighbor, to join him in celebrating these victories.

The Grand Master naturally understood the implications beneath the elegant surface of the letter. He sent back a reply listing the victories that the blue-blooded knights had enjoyed against their Muslim opponents, and asked the sultan to join *him* in celebration.

Suleiman responded with another letter. This one was a good deal more straightforward:

> I order you to hand over the island immediately. I recognize the right of you and your subordinates to leave the island with your valuables.

He went on to say that he would allow the Knights of St. John to remain on the island if they so desired, under the condition that they become his retainers. The 57-year-old Grand Master sent no reply.

War had been declared.

Chapter Four

On the Eve of the Battle

The Engineer Martinengo

For Antonio del Carretto, staying at the Italian knights' residence meant the beginning of a completely different life from that he had lived in his monastery near Genoa. Those who joined the Order of the Knights of St. John were normally required to train for three years at a monastery. Before serving as the "warriors of Christ," they were required to spend a number of years in frugality and peace as His servants in God. Antonio's training, however, ended after only one year because he was summoned by the order's headquarters on Rhodes, which was rushing to expand its military strength. Even his standard training, which all new recruits were supposed to receive, was postponed by direct order of the Grand Master.

The so-called standard training consisted of participating in attacks at sea on Muslim ships. It wasn't so much training as sudden immersion in real combat, but it was deemed necessary. Although the "blue bloods" had been trained to fight since childhood, few had fought aboard ship. Their vocation at Rhodes was that of pirate, and they needed to master the trade as quickly as possible.

Antonio's initial assignment was as an interpreter. He was to facilitate communication between the Venetian who had arrived on the same vessel as himself and the leaders of the order, including the Grand Master. It was not that the Grand Master and the leaders of the divisions, which were organized by language, could not understand Italian. The Venetian himself understood some French and German. His spoken Italian, however, was not the dialect of Venice but rather of neighboring Veneto. It was difficult for non-Italians to understand, and the Grand Master wished to understand all the subtle shades of meaning in the man's words. Antonio was born and raised in the Liguria region bordering on France and was thus bilingual in Italian and French. This was why he was chosen to act as interpreter.

The fact that the Grand Master didn't want to miss a single word the Venetian spoke gave Antonio the sense that the arrival of the commoner was more eagerly anticipated than that of ten or even a hundred knights. The man from Bergamo—a Venetian protectorate in northern Italy—was an engineer who specialized in the construction of fortifications.

His real name was Gabriele Tadino. Since he was born in the town of Martinengo on the outskirts of the city of Bergamo, his colleagues, architectural engineers, knew him simply as "Martinengo." He was in his late forties, was not an aristocrat, and was of sturdy built though short of stature.

He was said to have been a technical officer in the Venetian army during his twenties. When Padua was besieged by troops of the Holy Roman Empire under Maximillian I during the 1509 war against the League of Cambrai—a conflict in which Venice fought multiple foes—"Martinengo" took part in the city's defense. Three years later, he served in the vanguard of the Venetian army, who were now the aggressors, as they assaulted Brescia. Injured and captured during that battle, he was released a year later in a prisoner exchange. Upon his return, the Venetian government appointed him to a special post as a colonel with the authority to lead troops. His duties naturally dealt with the engineering of fortifications, and he continued to serve in that capacity for an additional three years in battles in northern Italy.

In 1516 the Venetian Senate dispatched him to oversee the fortifications of Crete, their largest base in the Aegean. For the next five years, as the supervising director of fortifications on Crete, Martinengo focused on maintaining and strengthening the fortresses of Grambusa, Canea, Souda, Retimo, Candia, and Spinalonga, which loomed from west to east along the northern coast of the island so that not even an ant could crawl through.

As Martinengo's sixth year on Crete approached, a young Frenchman secretly paid a visit to his residence in the capital city of Candia. The visitor introduced himself as La Vallette. He said he was a knight of the Order of St. John and had come from Rhodes. He then launched into a discussion that slowly made the Venetian engineer grow pale.

La Vallette brought word that the Grand Master wanted Martinengo to serve as director of fortifications on the Isle of Rhodes, but the knight hardly made a winning case. Quite to the contrary, he explained that a Turkish assault was inevitable, and that when it came the defenders would surely face a desperate battle. He also said nothing of the order's magnificent military successes against the heathens. He simply told Martinengo very clearly in calm, measured tones of the order's need for an expert engineer. This was sufficient to pique Martinengo's professional curiosity.

Martinengo had spent a long time on Crete, which was close to the front line in the struggle against the Turks, and knew that the sultan's determination to eradicate the Knights of St. John was stronger than ever. Yet he also knew that the Republic of Venice had made clear from the beginning its intention to remain neutral in the conflict between the Turks and the Knights. In fact the Governor of Crete, by order of the home government, had refused the Knights' requests to recruit mercenaries and purchase provisions on the island. Though Martinengo was an engineer, he was also a member of the Venetian army, and a colonel no less; accepting the order's invitation meant flaunting state policy. He knew that the Republic of Venice put its own interests above all else and would never permit its citizens to act against them. The governor was sure to turn down his request if Martinengo sought formal permission; at the same time, there was no specific directive that fortification engineers with Venetian citizenship should not collaborate with the Order of St. John. The offer to supervise the technical aspects of defending Rhodes in the imminent battle, which seemed destined to become a siege, appealed to Martinengo's professional pride.

Venetian engineers, whether they were fortification engineers or shipwrights, did not consider a job finished when the design and construction phases were complete. A ship engineer sailed into combat on the vessel of his fashioning and assumed total responsibility for handling repairs during transit and before and after the battle. Likewise, the skills of a fortification engineer were most needed during a siege. The split-second decisions of a single engineer could tip the tide of battle.

Martinengo had not designed the fortifications on Rhodes. Yet the engineer the order had employed three years earlier to carry out the large-scale rebuilding project was a fellow Venetian citizen named Scola, from the province of Vicinanza. Scola had completely renovated the defenses, and they were praised as the sturdiest in all of the Eastern Mediterranean. Those defenses were about to come under Martinengo's stewardship. He was just entering the prime of life, and the prospect must have filled him with a sweet agony.

It seems the young knight's unique enticement succeeded in the end. Martinengo told La Vallette he had no choice but to flee Crete. He intended to desert the Venetian military. La Vallette nodded, as if he had foreseen this possibility, and said, "We'll have a ship waiting for you in the Bay of Canea. You'll have to procure a small boat to reach it."

Martinengo replied that he could depart by boat from Canea harbor under the pretense of surveying the fortifications on Grambusa Island. He decided it would be advantageous to take two of his assistants with him, both to disguise his flight and to help with his tasks on

Rhodes. The escape took place nearly two months later. During that time, Martinengo passed many sleepless nights worrying that his plan might be discovered before it could be carried out. Even if he succeeded in escaping, the Venetian government would surely seek to punish him.

The day came and the Genoese ship carrying Antonio met up with Martinengo and his two assistants in their small boat. Once it was clear the danger had passed, Martinengo spent two full days collapsed in his berth, recovering from the mental strain. There was something, however, the engineer didn't know: shortly after he and his two assistants were brought aboard the Genoese ship, a message was sent east from the fortress at Canea by horse. Once the Governor of Crete received the message in Candia, he dispatched a clipper to Venice with a report.

The top-secret report from the governor was addressed to the head of the Council of Ten, the apex of the Venetian Republic's intelligence apparatus. The message read: "Technical Colonel Gabriele Tadino di Martinengo has successfully executed an escape."

A Farsighted Plan

Venice's survival depended on trade with other nations. Had the other nations of the world shared Venice's economic system, international affairs would have been dictated by economic principles alone. The reality was hardly that simple. States possessing ample territory could be self-sufficient when necessary and thus had trouble understanding the Venetian way of life rooted in commerce. Since the Venetians had no qualms about developing economic ties with followers of other religions, they were often considered unscrupulous and materialistic. This criticism was somewhat justified since the Muslims had made quite clear their intention to invade Christian lands. Venice was aiding and abetting the enemy.

The early sixteenth century was furthermore a time when the leadership of Western Europe was decisively shifting from Italian city-states like Venice to large territorial states such as France and Spain. A polity like Venice had to carry out its affairs with great caution if it wanted to survive in the new international environment. Such was the fate of a political entity whose very existence depended on its talent for diplomacy.

During the siege of Constantinople in 1453, the Venetian settlement in that city had accepted the Byzantine Emperor's request to help defend against the Turkish assault. The Venetians had fought openly under the Venetian flag. Nevertheless, immediately after the fall of Constantinople and the consequent demolition of the Byzantine Empire, Venice sent a special envoy to the new Turkish ruler of the city in the hopes of reestablishing a Venetian settlement to renew commercial ties. The envoy forced the Venetian citizens who had survived the battle to say that they had fought in a personal capacity; the official line was that the city-state deplored their actions. Yet none of the Venetians who died in that battle felt they had died in vain, and indeed they had not.

The magnificent millennium-long history of the Eastern Roman Empire came to an end with the fall of Constantinople. When the Ottoman Empire appeared in its place, the much-anticipated shift in the balance of power in the Mediterranean world toward Islam became a reality. In that campaign, the Venetians were the only Western Europeans who had raised their flag in defense. The Republic of Venice fully exploited this fact in its dealings with the pope and the rest of Christendom, while simultaneously making every effort to reestablish commercial ties with the infidel Turks. Had the Venetian settlement in Constantinople taken the same ambivalent attitude as that of the Genoese settlement, the republic never would have been able to walk this tightrope. Indeed, Venice reopened trade relations with the Turks long before Genoa.

Western European Christians viewed the destruction of a Christian empire by the Muslims as a grave and momentous event. They could not easily forgive Venice for fraternizing with those who had spilled Christian blood, especially before that blood had even had a chance to dry. Isolation seemed inevitable for Venice amidst this staunch chorus of criticism; isolation, however, was the one luxury a trading city like Venice couldn't afford. Venice was able to avoid the fate thanks to citizens who had spilled their blood in defense of the Byzantine capital.

The "desertion" of the engineer on Crete was also a product of the Venetian Republic's cunning sense of diplomacy.

The Venetians had little to gain from provoking the Turks, the significant other to the east. The republic had declared its neutrality. At the same time, the Turks' target in this case was the Isle of Rhodes, the base of the Order of the Knights of St. John, who were directly affiliated with the Roman Catholic Church. If Venice ignored Rhodes's plight, its inaction would be condemned by the pope and all of Christendom.

It was true that Venice had not allowed the order to procure provisions or recruit troops on Crete. Such conspicuous activities would be impossible to conceal from the Turks. They did not care, however, if an engineer in the Venetian army deserted his post and participated in the defense of Rhodes. They could tell the Turks he had deserted of his own volition, while the Europeans could be told that the so-called deserter was Venice's contribution to the war effort.

A fortification specialist was absolutely necessary in the case of a siege, and Venice had the most advanced fortifications in Europe at the time. Moreover, Martinengo was a technical officer of the highest rank on Crete, Venice's largest base in the Eastern Mediterranean. He was therefore as valuable as several ships loaded with provisions or soldiers. It even seems possible that the visit by La Vallette was itself somehow a clever ruse arranged by the republic. It was certainly something of which they were capable though there are no historical records to prove it.

Martinengo, however, believed he had risked death by deserting, and the regret that he had betrayed the republic burned in his chest for many years. He may be considered one of the victims of Venice's diplomatic strategy of deceiving its allies in order to deceive the enemy.

My Uncle, the Knight

The Venetian engineer's gracious reception by the knights completely violated their tradition of treating non-nobles as barely human. Grand Master L'Isle-Adam and the head of each knight's residence all had the impeccable posture of aristocrats, yet they leaned in to catch Martinengo's every word. The engineer spoke with the concise and lucid language of one confident in his technical expertise, offering his exact observations, analysis, and opinion. It was Antonio's job to translate all of it into French.

The Grand Master entrusted Antonio with this task not only because the young man understood both French and the Veneto dialect, but also because he was the nephew of the previous Grand Master, Fabrizio del Carretto, who had died serving the order. The Grand Master genuinely wanted Antonio to feel the greatness of his uncle's legacy.

In fact, it was not until their survey of the fortifications that Antonio truly came to feel the presence of the man he had known in the del Carretto family simply as his "uncle, the knight." Antonio had only met his uncle once at the age of ten. Fabrizio had been in charge of a detachment of the knights when the order provided security at the Lateran Council convened by Pope Julius II. Afterwards Fabrizio had stayed in Finale Castle for just a few days.

At that time, however, Uncle Fabrizio hardly had the air of a military commander. On the contrary, his behavior was as tranquil as a scholar's, which greatly disappointed the ten-year-old Antonio. Fabrizio would describe hand-to-hand combat with Muslim soldiers when asked to but relayed the events with such detachment that they might as well have happened to someone else. The assembled listeners, who had expected gripping tales of adventure, felt disappointed even if they weren't wide-eyed young boys.

When Antonio's father, the Marquis, introduced his three sons to Fabrizio, he proclaimed that the eldest would be the heir and that the youngest would serve in the army. Antonio, the second son, would follow in the footsteps of his uncle, the knight. The knight from the Order of St. John turned and looked gently upon his ten-year-old nephew. Antonio was only a child, but he was given the seat next to his uncle at the dinner table.

In the following year, 1513, when the news that Fabrizio had been selected as the next Grand Master reached the castle on the shore of the tranquil coast of Finale, the entire del Carretto family was astounded. None of them had imagined he would assume the mantle of leadership of one of Western Europe's most prestigious orders, much less one traditionally dominated by the French. The majority of Grand Masters had in fact been French. It had been forty years since an Italian had been selected. *That* appointment had seemed perfectly natural since the man in question had been a member of the Orsini family, one of the finest in Rome. To be selected from a line of marquises from the Genoese outskirts was quite another matter and was considered an epochal event. The pope even sent a letter of congratulations from Rome, and the topic of their uncle the new Grand Master dominated the family's conversation for a whole year.

As the years passed, this point of Italian pride was brought up less and less often. Fabrizio del Carretto served as Grand Master from 1513 to 1521, but there were no Turkish attacks during that time, and thus no illustrious stories of valor reached Europe. Even in the castle on the coast of Finale, he came to be mentioned less and less frequently. His name only resurfaced at large the year he died. Antonio was nineteen at the time, and by then wearing a monk's habit with a white cross on his chest—the mark of the Order of the Knights of St. John.

Now, a year later, Antonio finally saw with his own eyes how his uncle had spent his eight years as Grand Master. He saw the rampart walls encircling the city of Rhodes built by his uncle while Europe forgot him.

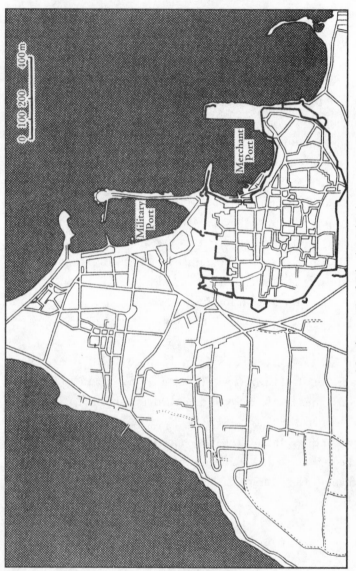

Northern tip of Rhodes Island

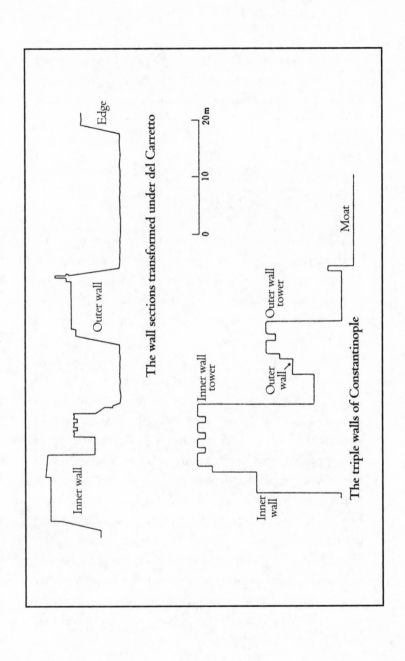

Edge

Outer wall

The wall sections transformed under del Carretto

20 m

10

0

Inner wall

Inner wall tower

Outer wall tower

Outer wall

Moat

Inner wall

The triple walls of Constantinople

Antonio's heart was set to burst with pride—which is why he didn't notice, not right away, the beaming admiration in the eyes of Martinengo, who was walking by his side as they proceeded around the top of the fortifications.

A City Fortress

The fortifications of the capital city of Rhodes did not encircle only the combatants, unlike the walls of Japanese castles of the feudal era. Following the precedent of most European cities, the walls were built around the entire city in order to protect the non-combatants as well, the average citizens.

The palace of the Grand Master, the residence halls of the various countries, as well as the hospital and armory were concentrated in the northern sector of the city; this area was set off by a wall. This was, however, a stone wall far too weak to offer significant protection and appears to have served only as a partition to divide the public from the private spheres of the city. The "fortress of Rhodes" acclaimed throughout the Mediterranean referred in fact to the fortifications surrounding the city itself.

The wall was approximately four kilometers long. If one included the projections that extended far out from the wall at strategic points, however, the length easily exceeded five kilometers. By long-standing tradition, each of the eight units of the order was responsible for a segment of the fortifications. They were to maintain and fortify their section in times of peace and to defend it in times of war.

The French unit from Ile-de-France was in charge of the 800 meters that began in the north at the Fort de Naillac. The stretch began at the entrance to the merchant port, passed the front of the military port and the northern section of the Grand Master's Palace, and then continued slightly to the south to the d'Amboise Gate. This gate was one of the city's only two land gates and bore the name of Grand Master Emery d'Amboise, who had reinforced the gate three terms ago. Although it served as a gate, it had such formidable and intricate defenses that it served as a part of the fortifications.

The 200 meters from the d'Amboise Gate to the Fort of St. Georges was the responsibility of the knights from Germany. At first sight this segment appeared quite short in comparison to the zone occupied by the French knights. The difference was not due to the differing numbers of men in the two contingents; the lowland facing the sea defended by the French was unsuitable for attack and in fact had never been assailed in the two hundred years since the order established its base on Rhodes. Conversely, the terrain from the d'Amboise Gate onward was all highlands and therefore incomparably more vulnerable to enemy assault.

The very design of the fortifications changed at the Gate d'Amboise, a fact that did not elude even Antonio's untrained eye. In the segment before the gate, the moat encircling the outer fortifications was narrow and the inner wall, faithful to traditional castle construction, soared high and straight. If the enemy were to assemble in this area, they would appear quite small from the walkway atop the battlements. One purpose of a castle was to intimidate those who drew near, and this section of the fortifications, capped by the towering height of the Grand Master's Palace, effectively fulfilled this function. The walls were especially awe-inspiring to those approaching by sea.

Beginning at the d'Amboise Gate, the appearance of the wall gradually began to change. The wall in this area was still tall with casemates at close intervals—parapets. These slots were suitable for a defense using bows or crossbows but were not spacious enough for cannons. At only four meters, the walls were quite thin. The moat alone was deep and wide. A stone bridge supported by three arches spanned the moat to connect the Gate d'Amboise to the grounds beyond.

The Fort of St. Georges was attached to the wall and looked like an octagon cut in half. It appeared midway along the long wall stretching almost in a straight line to the south. The Auvergne unit was responsible for the 300-meter section of wall from this massive protrusion to the Spanish (Aragonese) Fort. The wall in this section was more than ten meters wide but significantly less tall. The width of the casemates in the parapet increased at this point, allowing the placement of light cannons. Another fort protruded from the straight wall, which, together with the Spanish Fort, was designed to allow defenders to assail the enemy from both the front and the sides.

The section of wall between the Spanish Fort and the English Fort, a 200-meter stretch, was defended by the Aragonese unit. The moat along this section widened to a span of 100 meters and within it was another thick, outer wall that created a dual fortification. This outer wall was connected to the English Fort to facilitate the delivery of reinforcements.

The English unit was in charge of the 400-meter section that stretched in a nearly straight line from the English Fort to the Fort of Koskinou. Along this wall, as well, the moat was about 100 meters wide and contained a second defensive wall. Although the fortifications here were buttressed by the outer wall, they were far more exposed than the inward folding section guarded by the Aragonese contingent; it was impossible for the English Fort and the Fort of Koskinou to assist in the defense of these 400 meters. A total of four towers protruded from the wall in this segment to compensate for the disadvantages of the straight-line configuration. A bridge extended from the English Fort across the moat, but this was used only during peacetime, and was constructed as a drawbridge so that it could be retracted when necessary.

The Provençal unit was responsible for the 500 meters between the Fort of Koskinou and the Fort of del Carretto, named after the man responsible for its construction. The Fort of Koskinou was of a solid and substantial build comparable to the d'Amboise Gate, since it housed the second of the two gates leading out of the fortress. The stretch did not extend in a straight line, yet a total of three small towers, of either circular or angular design, protruded from the wall in order to compensate for the lack of a second wall outside it.

The Italian unit managed the area from the Fort of del Carretto to the levee embankment protecting the east side of the merchant harbor. The fortifications in this section, which was 400 meters long, comprised a two-layer defense with an outer wall in the moat. The design of the Fort of del Carretto completely disregarded what had been the standard castle-building technique—constructing towers of impressive height—and instead created the impression of a squat structure sitting low to the ground. Although the structure was built five hundred years before our times, it is best described by our contemporary term "bunker"—rather than "tower." Since its parapet walls were designed primarily to house cannons, they were also built low and looked impervious to even a heavy barrage of cannon fire. It was in, fact, the first tower of its type ever attempted. Antonio was speechless with wonder, while the specialist Martinengo was so impressed that he practically purred with satisfaction.

The fortifications along the border of the merchant harbor stretched for over 800 meters and were guarded by the unit from Castile. The Turkish navy was characterized by overwhelming numbers but also by inferior sailors, which ruled out an attack from sea. The Turkish navy's primary duty was transporting troops, so a seaward defense was unnecessary as long as there was no blockade. Given the Turks' lack of maritime expertise, there was little reason to fear such a contingency. The tall and thin fortifications, though dating from an era before the advent of large cannons, could safely be left as they were.

There was in addition a reserve force that could be dispatched at short notice to reinforce those sections of the landward wall where the enemy was bound to concentrate its attack. The unit was composed of knights of the Castilian and French units defending the seaward fortifications. The Grand Master of the Order himself led this unit. This tactic of the Knights of St. John meant that the mobile reserve force was destined to share in bearing the brunt of any attack.

That evening, in a spacious room facing the sea on the top floor of the Grand Master's Palace, the great wrought-iron chandelier hanging down from the ceiling shone brightly with all its candles lit. The twelve leather chairs arranged around a long wooden table in the center of the room were already filled. Martinengo had not offered many opinions during their survey of the fortifications; he had merely listened to the explanations and asked questions. Now, however, it was his turn to speak. After the survey, which had lasted until noon, the Venetian engineer had spent the afternoon cooped up in his lodgings in the Italian residence drafting numerous plans that were now stacked upon the room's table.

Grand Master L'Isle-Adam sat at the head of the brightly lit table, and Martinengo was assigned a seat directly opposite. Antonio, the interpreter, was seated to the engineer's left, and the heads of the knightly residences occupied the seats in between. To the left of the Grand Master sat Lieutenant Grand Master Dal Mare, head of the Castilian residence. To the right sat the Grand Master's secretary La Vallette, whose face remained as stern as ever. The deliberative council of the Order of St. John had gathered to hear the expert's opinion.

Cannon Versus Castle Wall

"The fortress appears to be even more magnificent than I had heard."

Antonio could sense that the engineer's words put everyone in the room at ease.

Weighing each of his words, Martinengo continued, "I am particularly impressed by how the latest techniques were applied in the areas where the brunt of the attack is expected. Castle builders such as myself have been suggesting such designs for decades, but nowhere has there been such a thoroughly realized example, not even in the Republic of Venice."

This tickled the pride of the leaders of the order, who did not care for Venice.

The patriotic Martinengo did not neglect to add:

"On the other hand, our republic controls many lands, and we cannot afford to commit our thoughts exclusively to a single fortress."

Venice's castle-building technology was considered the state of the art, and Germany, France and Spain were enthusiastically recruiting Venetian engineers. It was understandable that the knights could barely conceal their delight when one of these engineers, a leading one at that, gave their fortress his seal of approval. The onslaught of the great Turkish army was becoming a pressing reality, and the defending army—with a core of six hundred knights and numbering only a few thousand—had nothing but the walls to rely on to hold off the Turks.

The fall of Constantinople in 1453 was a historical event that marked the beginning of inevitable social and military transformations in both East and West. These upheavals were so far-reaching that they ushered in a new era, but, for the same reason, the changes were not so immediate that they could be felt just a year or two after the event. While there had been a number of people who were painfully aware of the need for change before Constantinople fell, it was impossible for them to achieve such reforms quickly unless they were tyrants with absolute power.

Many already realized that Sultan Mehmed II's use of cannons had been a crucial factor in deciding the battle for Constantinople. An Italian expert in castle design from Sienna published an essay only two years after the siege that dealt with adapting fortification engineering to the new age of cannons. Indeed, at the end of the fifteenth century, Leonardo da Vinci designed a fortress specifically with defense against cannons in mind; the Sangallo family, who were famous builders and designers, also published a number of tentative plans. For a number of reasons, it took more than half a century before such fortresses were built.

First of all, after toppling Constantinople, the Ottoman Empire temporarily directed its might further north, partly because its navy had been weakened. Those living in the south in and around the Mediterranean did not perceive a direct threat from the Turks during that time. Second, Venice, the power on the front line of European Christendom against the Turks, had a republican system of government. Unlike a dictatorship, a republic needs time to deliberate on proposed courses of action. Moreover, applying cannon-oriented technology to improve the fortresses on their numerous bases from the Adriatic to the Aegean was an immense undertaking that required spending vast sums of money over a long period. A single council could not initiate such a sea change in priorities; the matter had to be put to the entire republic. More than a few people had to become involved. At least half of those responsible for setting policy had to be convinced of the necessity of such a major project, or it would never happen. Yet these decision-makers were unlikely to realize the importance of the project unless large numbers of them were in imminent danger.

It was thus not until the end of the fifteenth century that Venetian fortifications began to change decisively. Venice initially recruited engineers from other parts of Italy while working enthusiastically to improve its own technology. The results of these efforts were first seen in the fortresses on the islands of Cyprus and Crete, which were right on the Ottoman "border."

Circumstances were a little different for the knights on Rhodes, who were arrayed with the Venetians on the Eastern Mediterranean front. The lands under the order's protection were neither as numerous nor as remote as those of the Venetians: no more than a handful of small surrounding islands in addition to Rhodes. Furthermore, the order was not organized as a republic. The Grand Master and the members of the high council, less than ten in number, made all the decisions. Often these decisions followed the will of the Grand Master alone. Compared to Venice, where the Doge's vote was just one of two thousand, it was an extremely nimble organization.

Nevertheless, reforms did not proceed easily. This was in part because the Turkish army didn't immediately set its sights on Rhodes. Like the Venetians, the knights didn't fully recognize the danger until it was imminent. In fact, the fortress walls on Rhodes in 1480, when Mehmed II suddenly dispatched a large army, were of the pre-cannon design typified by the walls of Constantinople; like those of the fallen city, the island capital's walls were relatively thin and rose straight from the ground. The central wall was only wide enough for a single archer, and towers occupied the key strategic points between the walls, which stood in straight lines. The island was successfully defended only because the Turkish generals took a passive strategy in the absence of their sultan and the troops were ravaged by an epidemic. Even the French knights, who thought of themselves as the personification of the old chivalric spirit, knew those walls wouldn't suffice in future battles.

The strengthening of the fortress walls on Rhodes began as soon as that battle had ended, thanks to the efforts of d'Aubusson and d'Amboise, two Grand Masters who refused to be intoxicated by victory. It was forbidden for Grand Masters who built new walls or fortified existing ones to inscribe them with their own crests, but those of d'Aubusson and d'Amboise can still be seen here and there.

Their reinforcements were a testament to the two men's great zeal, but that was the extent of their efforts. Perhaps they found it impossible to break free of the traditional conception of a fortress. The fortress walls on Rhodes certainly became sturdy, but vestiges of the medieval castle still clearly lingered around it. Perhaps, in order to transform their castle, they had to wait for an Italian to come along, as Italians were the most pragmatic people of the age.

Fabrizio del Carretto, Grand Master of the Order for eight years between 1513 and 1521. Several records indicate that he had plans to radically reform the fortress walls as soon as he took up the post. Five years would pass

before he set about the task—five years that were most
likely spent securing funding. Surviving construction
account ledgers in Venice show that the building of a
fortress required eye-popping monetary resources.

Grand Master del Carretto made three visits to
recruit the castle engineer Basilio della Scola, who was
famous even in Venice. Since the Turks hadn't yet made
clear their intention to attack the Knights of St. John, the
Venetians, who had once again established friendly relations with the Turks, did not fuss over sending the Knights
one of their most gifted engineers. The Republic of Venice
was open-minded about providing "technological assistance" of this sort as long as it didn't cause problems on
the diplomatic front. As a result, the engineer Scola was
able to arrive in grand style on the Isle of Rhodes in the
light of day. He remained there for three years.

Scola's plan for reform was revolutionary. When his
blueprints were shown to the French knights, many
protested to Grand Master del Carretto that they couldn't
bring themselves to fight in such an unsightly fortress.
Scola's planned fortifications were completely different
from traditional walls such as those of Constantinople,
which towered straight from the ground. His plan
emphasized digging over building. Walls had traditionally been designed to allow soldiers to face off against an
enemy on land from as high a position as possible;
according to Scola's proposal, the attackers and the
defenders would be set against each other at roughly the
same height. The moats that separated them were also

altered, becoming much deeper and wider than before. In other words, no matter what kind of cannon fire they drew, they could tenaciously hold their ground. These reforms were most boldly applied to the landward walls which would inevitably bear the brunt of the enemy's attack. The northern and northeastern walls facing the military and merchant ports remained almost entirely untouched, since those could be defended as they were so long as the ones doing the attacking were the nautically inept Turks.

Scola didn't destroy the foundations of the old walls. Rather, he reduced their height, which yielded earth, sand, and stones, which he then used in conjunction with new building stones to thicken the walls dramatically. The walkways on top of the walls were widened to ten meters all the way along the western and southern sides. Even the inner walls at Constantinople, which were said to have been the strongest in the world, had been no more than five meters wide. Yet Scola, still not satisfied, also had additional support buttresses built inside the walls. These were diagonally sloping stone walls that supported the fortress walls from within. With the exception of those points where stone staircases had been built along the side of the walls, the segments defended by the divisions from Auvergne, Aragon, England, Provence, and Italy were all reinforced from the inside in this fashion. The looming towers, which appeared so medieval, were not destroyed either. Rather, they too were lowered, and the ones in tactically important locations were reinforced with building stones.

In Italian, a parapet with casemates is called a *merli*, which is derived from the word for "lace," because notches are lined along the tops of the wall just like the fringe of a piece of lace. Scola also changed this medieval design to a *merloni*, which can only be translated as "great lace," that is, a "great parapet." This was done everywhere along the wall except in certain locations. The advantage of changing the parapets into *merloni* was that, even if they came under cannon fire, they would resist breaking into pieces.

In addition, in front of the walls defended by the divisions from Aragon, England, and Italy, where the moat widened significantly, an outer stone wall was built in the moat. It was safer to be far from the enemy, but it also made it more difficult to inflict damage upon the enemy. The defenders would thus begin the siege at the outer walls, from which they could retreat if the situation worsened. From the outer wall girding the Spanish wall, it was possible to escape into the English Fort. In a pinch, troops protecting the outer wall in front of the main post of the English section could retreat to the English Fort or the Koskinou Fort, from where they could move to defend the inner wall. The outer wall in front of the Italian section led to del Carretto's Fort.

The moat was dug twenty meters deeper than the grounds where enemy troops were expected to assemble, and extended a good twenty meters beyond even the outer walls. The moat was thus capacious enough so that not even the Turkish army, which attacked in "human waves," would find it easy to fill. Constantinople's moat had also been twenty meters wide but, being only a meter deep, had wound up being quickly filled. Widening the moats any further would not have offered a tactical advantage since fighting became impossible past a certain range. The Knights of St. John, who were not connected by land to any allies, needed to avoid a prolonged siege at all costs. The moat at Rhodes could not be filled with seawater because the sea level was too low. Digging any deeper to allow this was impractical as it risked flooding the city.

But the most significant characteristic of Scola's re-engineering was probably the protrusions, known in military terminology as bastions, which jutted out abruptly from the main fortress walls.

I have used the very loose "fort" rather than the technical "bastion." Bastions are not free-standing structures apart from the main castle walls; forts, according to the dictionary, are small-scale strongholds built separately from the main castle. The problem is that "English Bastion" or "Bastion of St. George" is not appropriate for telling the story of this siege which took place in the early sixteenth century. Also, I wrote of "towers" in my book *The Fall of Constantinople*, but for reasons that I am about to touch upon, the "bastions" of Constantinople and those of Rhodes were quite different in character.

The "bastions" of Rhodes acted more or less as forts. As long as they remained standing, the main fortress walls would not fall. The reader should imagine

that forts defended the strategic points along the exten-
sive walls.

In other words, the tall, square towers placed at forty-
meter intervals along the walls of Constantinople were not
to be found in Rhodes. Instead, huge forts thrust out from
the main walls in each of the zones assigned to the various
divisions. The towers in the siege of Constantinople, simply square and tall, had not served as a key element in the
defense. There, the only difference between holding the
walls and the towers was that the latter were taller and
allowed the use of their two lateral sides. Since towers
were not seen as terribly useful, the defenders had not even
utilized the advantages that they did offer.

On Rhodes, in contrast, the multi-sided "forts"
were considered essential. That was why each division
had one. Once a siege had begun in earnest, the commander of each division—on Rhodes, this meant the
Master of each residence—would barricade himself
within the fort and lead the battle from there. The division flags were unfurled atop each of these forts.

It was impossible to sustain the defense of an entire
section of the wall, which could be anywhere from 200
to over 400 meters long, from a single fort. For that reason, smaller forts were placed at approximately 100-
meter intervals. Since the area that could be covered from
a square building was limited, these smaller forts were
multi-sided or round.

These reforms were clearly adopted because they
were thought to compensate for the knights' numerical

disadvantage. The history of castle building in the West over the next hundred years would revolve around the progressive development of these bastions. When he died, Fabrizio del Carretto left behind a fortified city that was of the highest standard possible for the beginning of the sixteenth century.

After Martinengo gave his expert opinion on the Rhodian fortress he said, "If dealing with cannons were the only issue, we could say that the walls here are perfect. Completing the reforms on the wall indicated on this diagram would be sufficient. It is certain, however, that the Turks will use mines. They tried to use them at Constantinople, but at that time they had no engineers skilled in tunneling. At this point, however, they have full-time units specializing in this."

Martinengo wasn't implying that Scola had neglected to take measures against explosives. It was quickly apparent to Martinengo, a fellow engineer, that Scola had been working on the issue. The very act of deepening the moat was meant to hinder enemy troops trying to dig tunnels underneath the fortress walls. Scola had additionally dug a one-meter-deep ditch running along the interior base of the main wall. This would enable the defenders to determine, on the basis of sound alone, where the enemy was trying to tunnel. If they could accurately guess where the enemy tunnel was aimed, the defenders could immediately dig a counter-tunnel to intercept it. It would be easy to fight the tunnelers back, after which it was only a matter of blowing up and blocking the tunnel. The Turkish army wouldn't resume work on a tunnel once it had been discovered.

Martinengo's proposals in this regard were no more than improvements on the existing system. He explained that the existing one-meter ditch was not deep enough, so they would have to dig further and then cover the top of the ditch with planks, like a roof. The reasoning was that if the top of the ditch were left open, it would eventually be filled in by the sand, earth, and stones blown in from all directions by cannon fire. This would render the ditch more or less useless.

The leaders of the order, from Grand Master on down, accepted all of Martinengo's proposals and decided to commence the project the following day. They would entrust him with overseeing the construction and provide him with all the laborers, supplies, and money he requested. Although only a "red blood," he was given full authority over the fortifications.

Martinengo thanked them but added the following words of caution: "No matter how impregnable the fortress, time is always on the side of the attackers."

The Knights of St. John knew this, of course, and were thinking of ways to address the matter. As soon as they had received the *de facto* declaration of war from Sultan Suleiman I, they had dispatched envoys to the Vatican and the courts of France and Spain requesting reinforcements. But times had changed too dramatically in Western Europe to hope for a Crusader army from a federation of Christian powers.

The battle of Constantinople in 1453 is a good example of how war can change history. The use of cannons forced a complete reform of subsequent castle design and tactics in general. The deployment of a massive army also urged a shift toward the age of monarchic states. In both these ways, the 1522 siege of Rhodes was the first war waged under the influence of what had occurred seventy years earlier. But few in Europe understood what was transpiring on the southern island.

The Roman Knight

That evening, Antonio del Carretto was relieved of his duties as interpreter. Once a concrete project like the maintenance of castle walls began, complicated ideas no longer needed to be exchanged. Whether Martinengo was using his Veneto-accented Italian, the rough Greek he had picked up while staying on Crete, or his smattering of German and French, the language barriers weren't enough to hinder the work.

Antonio was nonetheless still unable to participate in the "piracy training" that novice knights normally underwent as soon as they arrived on Rhodes. The order was preparing for the looming Turkish attack and couldn't spare even a single ship. In fact, they had earlier called off all attacks on Turkish vessels. Ships flying the flag of the order continued to leave the port in the morning and return in the evening, but only to patrol the surrounding waters. There had been few recent sightings of Turkish ships. The Muslims, too, were beginning to sense the war clouds on the horizon.

Despite that, the Isle of Rhodes was bustling with energy. Countless cargo ships brimming with provisions and ammunition entered the merchant port every day. In the military port, the sound of hammers repairing galleys rang until sunset. Landside, native Rhodian men had been mobilized, and the process of enhancing the fortress walls was underway. Martinengo slept like the dead after returning to the Italian knights' residence in the evening, evidence of the fullness of his days as the engineer in charge.

The leaders of the order spent many successive days busily addressing unresolved problems, but the younger knights without posts had little to do aside from their weekly responsibilities at the hospital. Upkeep of armor and weapons was performed by the valets who had accompanied them from their home countries. Antonio wondered why Orsini was nowhere to be seen among the many knights using this time to polish their skills at the sword or crossbow.

Antonio hadn't seen Orsini since encountering him on the staircase that first morning at the Grand Master's Palace. Remembering how Orsini had given him an open invitation, Antonio decided to pay a visit to this man with the somewhat scandalous reputation.

Finding Giambattista Orsini's home was an unexpectedly difficult task for Antonio, who had just arrived
on Rhodes. Many of the veteran knights, who were
allowed to live outside of the residences, chose to rent
houses in the part of town where the inns of various
countries were concentrated, but Orsini wasn't one of
them. Antonio searched and searched until he finally
arrived at his destination, a neighborhood located
between the Italian wall and the merchant port—as far
away from the other knights as it was possible to get.
Not even Greeks born on Rhodes lived there. It was a
place settled by Italians staying on Rhodes for business,
and Jews, who were found everywhere across the
Mediterranean.

The house was in the Rhodian style, small but com-
fortable, with a courtyard thick with vegetation. The
refreshing breezes particular to Rhodes gently caressed
one's skin everywhere throughout the house. The door
was opened by an old valet, taciturn but the very picture
of integrity, whom Orisini had brought along from his
estate in the north of Rome and whom Antonio had
previously met at the Italian knights' residence.

The stone staircase in the courtyard led up to a
cloister on the second floor that was gracefully supported by round, slender pillars. The young Roman knight
was leaning against one of those pillars, waiting for him.
He was not wearing his silver-gleaming suit of armor,

but rather a loose-fitting white hemp shirt that was casually tucked into thin black tights, the string at his chest untied. It was with some irritation that Antonio struggled not to let Orsini's relaxed reception affect him.

The Roman knight indicated a chair in the sun-lit elevated corridor. This seemed to be an invitation to sit. Orsini sat on a Turkish divan, on which he appeared to have been sitting before Antonio's arrival, and stretched out his legs. His way of reclining on his side with his upper body supported by cushions and his legs outstretched reminded Antonio of the sculptural reliefs he had often seen on Etruscan tombs back in Italy.

"I hear the leaders have released you from your duties. Aren't you bored?"

Antonio found himself smiling, and Orsini seemed to take that as an answer. Just then, the sound of something like soft Greek music, a voice, came from behind Antonio's back. Turning around, he saw a woman with a jar filled with the favorite drink of everyone who lived on Rhodes, lemon water mixed with honey. She was the reason for Orsini's bad reputation. Even Antonio could recognize the difference between a woman who just happened to be visiting and one who actually lived there. For a knight in a religious order that observed vows of chastity, obedience, and poverty, living with a woman was of course a problem.

Not that all of the knights observed all of the vows. Only the vow of obedience was strictly upheld. As for poverty, living on Rhodes seemed in itself to fulfill the vow for the sons of illustrious European nobility. Compared to the lifestyles of their brothers back in Europe, which consisted of days spent in the courts of kings and in castles on their own estates, life on Rhodes certainly resembled poverty. Marriage was naturally forbidden, but secret dalliances were overlooked. Orsini was the only knight, however, who lived with a woman openly.

She was a native of Rhodes. She had been married to a Greek merchant who had, several years earlier, disappeared after heading off for Constantinople. For the past two years, rumors had circulated about her relationship with Orsini. The husband's family was said to be deeply ashamed of her; she was no longer welcome in the Greek part of town. Antonio learned all this some time later from his own valet. Rumors spread quickly among the valets.

The woman gathered her rich, wavy black hair at the nape of her neck. Her well-defined features, in contrast to those of Italian women, conveyed an impression of strength rather than gentleness. Yet the way she carried her slender body as she poured drinks from the jar into silver cups was breathtakingly graceful. Her demeanor was neither self-deprecating nor coarse. She knew her position and acted accordingly in a very natural way, and the faint smile she offered as she waited on her guest put Antonio truly at ease. She was not young. She looked to be the same age as Orsini—twenty-five, Antonio had heard—or older. The young del Carretto was certain he had never seen such a natural, unstrained pairing of man and woman. A sweet pleasure overcame him as his initial discomfort faded away.

From his second visit on, Antonio made the trip to Orsini's unaccompanied by his valet. There were times when he and Orsini would speak indoors, but they frequently spent time out in the roofed hallway until nightfall, just as they had that first time. It was nearly summer. The Greek woman was present at every visit. It seemed that tasks outside of the home were the responsibility of Orsini's valet.

Antonio and Orsini were both Italians and members of the same class, so there was no shortage of polite conversation between them. At some point during his third visit, though, Orsini suddenly looked Antonio straight in the eye and asked him, "Do you think Europe will send reinforcements?"

Antonio could not answer. Everyone in the Italian residence spoke as if the reinforcements had already set sail, but Antonio couldn't shake a vague sense of anxiety.

"The reinforcements aren't coming," said Orsini. "Europe is not in a position to send help to a southern island like this one. We have no choice but to fight as if we've been abandoned."

Antonio was at a loss for words. The Roman knight gazed at him with kindness and then turned his eyes to the top of a cypress tree towering in the courtyard. He continued:

"I live right next to the merchant port and hear the reports firsthand. I hear all of the news that gets filtered out as it passes from the merchant port to the Grand Master's Palace and finally down to us.

"We are a formal religious order recognized by the pope, and thus are under his direct jurisdiction. The standard procedure for requesting reinforcements is for us to send envoys to the pope in Rome. After the pope hears our request, he sends a personal letter to all the kings and princes, encouraging them to participate, and they in turn provide troops who gather under the papal flag. The Crusader armies, after all, were meant to defeat the infidels, and they were always assembled in this way. Regardless of how any given king may burn with the Crusader spirit, and even if he actually has the power to contribute troops, his plan for a Crusade cannot be put into action without the approval of the pope. This is quite a different matter from defending one's own territory.

"Incidentally, and I think you are already aware of this, Pope Leo X from the House of Medici suddenly passed away early last December. No one had expected this, as he was only forty-five; the Vatican no doubt fell into a great panic. The cardinals apparently hadn't given much thought to who should be pope next, so an entire month passed before they could manage to convene a conclave.

"But this lack of preparation set the stage for disunity among the most powerful cardinals. No matter how many times they met, none of the cardinals was able to obtain two-thirds of the vote, necessary to be elected pope. Desperation must have driven someone to nominate a cardinal who was far away and unable to arrive in time for the conclave. He was considered a scholar and man of integrity. Knowing how uncooperative Italians can be, it's easy to imagine that both sides of the split were eager to throw their votes behind the foreigner—better that than having your rival selected. This is how we Catholic believers came to have a Dutch pope about whom we know nothing except that he was the tutor of Charles, the Holy Roman Emperor.

"But the new pope, who was in the Spanish lands to which he had been assigned, could not set off for Rome immediately upon receiving the news. That is why he is still in Spain, even though he made his first official declaration of acceptance in February this year. At that time he also announced that the two major challenges facing the Catholic Church were dealing with the Lutheran movement and unifying the Christian states to form an anti-Muslim Crusader army. But until he has the tiara placed upon his head, he is not yet officially the pope. The coronation ceremony is held in the Church of St. Peter in Rome, and the Vatican has no choice but to continue with a vacant throne until that happens. In other words, the Vatican's hands will continue to be tied.

"In any event, I have heard that the question of the route the new pope should take from Spain to Rome is turning into a problem. The Holy Roman Emperor Charles says he wants to celebrate the promotion of his childhood tutor together with all of his subjects. He therefore wants the pope to travel by sea from Spain, which is under his control, to the Netherlands, which is also under his control, and from there to Italy through Germany—yet again, territory under his control. I imagine the emperor's real motive is to prevent his rival, the King of France—with whom he is on very poor terms—from getting close to the new pope. If the pope passes through France, protocol dictates that he meet the king.

"They say that England's Henry VIII also sent an envoy to the new pope, suggesting that he sail from Spain to England, and cross from there over into the Netherlands. The French King François I of course recommended a route that passed through France.

"The new pope, for his part, has apparently decided to go by sea from Spain to Genoa, then again by sea to Rome's outer port of Ostia. This route enables him to avoid snubbing or hurting the feelings of the emperor or the French and British kings. But he hasn't departed yet because the Vatican has no navy and can't send a ship to fetch him. Under these circumstances, the Catholic Church doesn't even know when it will have its leader.

"But even if the pope were in place, and even if he wanted with all his heart to eradicate the infidels, do you really think it would make any difference?"

"No, I don't think it would," answered Antonio. "The Lutheran sect has been active for two years now, ever since Luther's excommunication. I'm sure the Vatican considers dealing with the sectarians its most serious challenge."

"Indeed," said Orsini. "Resolving that issue is the

one problem the new pope can't put off. The common people are restless, even in those countries where Protestantism has yet to penetrate. Even if a cynic like myself were to become pope, that would be the first problem I would confront. No matter how you look at it, dealing with the heathen Turks comes second on the list.

"We have Spain, where unification was achieved through the marriage of the monarchs of Castile and Aragon; France, where authority was more centralized than anywhere else in Europe; England, where domestic unification moved forward after their continental ambitions were thwarted; Germany, where the power of the elected princes held centralization back, even though there was a figure like the Holy Roman Emperor, who stood above various national monarchs; and Italy, which is divided into Milan, Venice, Florence, the Vatican, and Naples. An odd relationship used to be maintained between all of these countries—not equilibrium per se, but no other word quite fits.

"That situation began to change little by little, and now it is about to change once and for all. The change began in the first place because of what the Turks were doing in the East. The fall of Constantinople and the destruction of the Byzantine Empire gave the Turkish people a just cause, namely the 'inheritance' of the territories that had once belonged to the former empire. The Turks capitalized on this, and now they are closing in on Vienna in the north, pushing up against Persia in the east after having crossed the Tigris and Euphrates rivers, and surrounding the Red Sea in the south. To the west, they control northern Africa from Egypt to Algeria. They are emerging as a great empire.

"Western Europe has no choice but to form larger states to meet the challenge of this offensive from the east. Just as it started to become clear what the era demanded, Charles fortuitously appeared.

"Six years ago, in 1516, Charles rose to the Spanish throne after the death of his maternal grandfather, King Ferdinand. He had inherited land in the Netherlands even before 1516 when his father Philip, heir to the Holy Roman Empire, died an early death. Three years ago, in 1519, the Holy Roman Emperor Maximilian died as well. As a result, Charles, a direct descendant of the Hapsburgs, also came to rule Germany and Austria.

"This marked the beginning of his reign as Holy Roman Emperor Charles V and Spanish King Charles I, whose dominion included the New World. He was born in 1500, which makes him twenty-two years old this year. Even if one hopes for this great empire to collapse with his death, it is not going to happen unless the goddess of fate plays an especially vicious trick. There is also not much hope that the Turkish Sultan Suleiman, at twenty-eight, will die soon.

"Furthermore, the ruler of France, François I, is flanked on both sides by the Hapsburgs and is growing increasingly wary. He took the throne in 1515 at the age of twenty-one, which makes him twenty-eight this year, the same age as Suleiman. England's king, Henry VIII, is thirty-one.

"Charles, Suleiman, François and Henry are not only young, but they are also all truly great monarchs. Under these circumstances, I think it's safe to speculate that a reorganization of Europe will proceed with increasingly decisive momentum.

"Conflict between Charles and François has already started in Italy. The land has become Spanish territory from Naples southward, but the two are fighting for control of Milan and the rest of northern Italy. In addition, the Republic of Florence is fully in France's shadow; its 'independence' is a mere charade. This being the case, the Republic of Venice is the last genuinely independent state in Italy. With a domestic situation such as this, the last thing the Venetians want is a confrontation with the Turks in the Eastern Mediterranean—even if it means standing by and watching Rhodes fall.

"This is a bird's-eye-view of Europe, the world we were born into. In a reality such as this, who do you suppose will send an expedition south to help the Knights of St. John conquer the infidels? The Spanish and the French have mobilized a total of 50,000 soldiers to wage war against one another in Italy. The kings of those two realms wouldn't dream of sending even a tenth that number to help us. We may belong to the same age as they, but they control the course of events in a way we do not. There is nothing for us now but to raise our solitary resistance here and die doing so."

One month later, Antonio set out to sea.

The Grecian Sea

Antonio was part of a group ordered by the Grand Master to conduct a final inspection of the fortresses on the order's outlying islands. Giambattista Orsini led the group, which consisted of five knights. Antonio presumed he was added to the group at Orsini's recommendation.

Their fast galley turned its prow west as soon as it left Rhodes's military port. They soon changed course to the northwest. The Aegean Sea ("the sea of many islands") lived up to its name: as soon as one island disappeared over the horizon, the next came into view. After traveling over 100 kilometers from Rhodes, they drew near Leros, the Knights' northernmost island.

Five knights were permanently stationed at the fort on Leros. The group from Rhodes was to take them, twenty Greek soldiers, and all of their weapons and ammunition, from Leros to the island of Kos, fifty kilometers to the south. The job of the contingent on Leros was to use signal fire relays to notify Kos whenever they discovered a southbound Turkish fleet. The fort on the island, however, was not sturdy enough to withstand an attack by a large army. The leaders of the order had decided it would make more sense to bolster the defenses on Kos.

Antonio and Orsini's galley went to Kos in advance of the others, before the loading was complete. Kos was a much larger island than Leros, but like Rhodes its defenses were concentrated on a fortress overlooking its northernmost harbor. Only ten kilometers separated this harbor from the western edge of Asia Minor looming on the opposite shore. All but the largest of vessels headed from Constantinople to Egypt or Syria had to navigate through the waters of this ten-kilometer channel.

This was such a valuable strait that the Knights had been holding on to the stretch of Asia Minor facing Kos for over a hundred years, even though it was only a tiny part of the opposite coast. Bodrum, twenty kilometers from Kos, was the best harbor in the area and it was where they had built their fortress. If small Muslim ships happened through the waters between Bodrum and Kos, ships stationed in these two harbors dealt with them. In the case of a larger fleet, word of approaching prey spread across the network of islands to Rhodes. Unless the Muslims sailed under the protection of a fleet of warships, it was impossible for them to sail unscathed through Rhodian waters.

Having finished their work on Kos, the group left for Bodrum, their only base on Asia Minor. Not only did it have the strongest fortress in the region, but also a well-fortified harbor with a shipyard where several attack galleys waited at the ready. After Rhodes, Bodrum was the most important base of the Order of the Knights of St. John. Not only was it strategically located for attacking Turkish ships, but it alone could function in another key capacity: it was where Christians enslaved by the Turks throughout Asia Minor could head if they were fortunate enough to escape. This was not a rare occurrence. As a religious order, the Knights of St. John performed the extremely important duty of offering protection to fugitive Christians and sending them to Rhodes before ultimately returning them to Europe.

Antonio unexpectedly found himself alone on the bridge with Orsini and took the opportunity to talk with him for the first time since they had set out. Orsini had been busy until that moment meeting with the knights manning the fort on Kos, and the mood had not been conducive to a personal exchange. Orsini himself seemed like a different man from the one who had spoken with such melancholy back in the exposed corridor of his overly breezy house; he now seemed like a commander eminently suited to issue one brisk order after another. When Antonio told him so, the young Roman knight replied with a bitter smile on his face:

"All human beings have the right to die without feeling their death was in vain. And it's the duty of their superiors to make them feel that way."

The two had another chance to be alone after their meal that evening. This time, Orsini invited Antonio to take a walk along the top of the fortress walls. Since Bodrum's fortress was built so that it extended out into the harbor's entrance, there was nothing before them but the sea sinking into the darkness of the night. The lights of fishermen's ships were visible to one side; some were slowly moving, while others remained motionless. The surface of the sea was still, like spilt oil. Naturally, the two men could feel the wind at the top of the walls. Off in the distance ahead of them, clusters of tiny flickering lights were visible. They were the lights of Kos. Had the people on Kos wanted to send signals with those lights, they would be readily deciphered from the fortress.

The two of them climbed to the top of one of the forts, commonly called the "Englishmen's Fort." English knights were by tradition responsible for Bodrum's defense. Antonio lost himself in thoughts he'd been nursing for some time, forgetting for a moment that Orsini was standing next to him.

He was thinking that Kos, which they had departed that morning, was the birthplace of Hippocrates, father of medicine; and that Herodotus, father of history, had been born in Bodrum, where he was standing at that moment. Bodrum had been called Halicarnassus in ancient times, and just a little to its north was Miletus. A little further up was Ephesus, and further north from there the ancient battlefield of Troy. If you turned your eyes to the sea just short of Troy, you could expect to see the island of Lesbos, home of the lyricists of antiquity.

The young man was at play in the world of ancient Greece. When Orsini's voice brought him back to his senses he felt somewhat unsettled, as if he had been forcefully dragged across a span of two thousand years. Antonio loved Orsini, but he was displeased with his friend's insensitivity to such things.

"After leaving Constantinople, the Turkish army will cross the Bosphorous Strait into Asia Minor. From there, I imagine they will head south after passing through Bursa en route to Smyrna. They will probably continue south from Smyrna until they arrive in Marmaris, which is only fifty kilometers across the sea from Rhodes. Marmaris is most likely where they will establish their main base, since the harbor at Marmaris is located at the heart of a complex bay where even our fast ships will be unable to attack.

"The Turkish navy, on the other hand, which consists mostly of troop transports, will pass through the Dardanelles into the Aegean Sea. They will then go south along the coast of Asia Minor, pass through these waters before us here, and then enter the harbor at Marmaris. Since it's a more pleasant trip, the Sultan may go by sea if he plans to lead the army personally. Either way, fleets of large warships will be passing through this narrow channel, so even if we lie in wait with our five warships, we'll simply be knocked aside.

"The Turkish army aims to conquer the Isle of Rhodes, so they surely won't waste time attacking small bases. Any effort to defend these small forts will prove meaningless if Rhodes falls; they will certainly ignore Kos and Bodrum and pass them by. It is therefore pointless to keep defenders on Kos or Bodrum, especially now, when every soldier and every cannonball is needed on Rhodes. All fortifications at these bases should be abandoned."

Antonio asked him why he hadn't suggested that to the Grand Master.

"I did, but the Grand Master said, 'We cannot let the Muslim flag fly over islands that our predecessors spent long years defending to the death.' My idea wasn't categorically dismissed, though. When the Grand Master's orders reached the knights on the islands beyond Rhodes, they promptly ordered their subordinates to abandon their fortifications and rush to the defense of Rhodes. After all, if the siege lasts two months, even the chivalrous French knights will appreciate a 30-man reinforcement."

Antonio, who was shocked to hear that the siege might last two months, asked if it could really carry on that long. Orsini answered, "We'll be lucky if it only lasts two months. I doubt we'll be that lucky."

He spoke in such a quiet tone that if Antonio had not been downwind, he wouldn't have been able to hear Orsini's sunken voice.

Eastward

Early in the morning two days later, their galley lifted anchor. They would be passing both Kos and Rhodes on their way to Kas, which was about a hundred kilometers further to the east. The fort there was the Knights' easternmost base. In other words, they ruled the seas from Leros to Kas.

As Antonio watched from the ship's stern, ancient Halicarnassus emerged in the light of morning. He saw in the hills just above the port the remnants of a semicircular theater, the stone rows of spectator seats, spread out like a fan, faced toward the sea. Had it been built in the Greek era or the Roman? In any event, this part of the Mediterranean had prospered, in every sense of the word, during antiquity.

It had once been called Ionia, Antonio recalled, and was the birthplace of philosophy. The quiet morning light bathed the towns along this brief stretch of water, which even a small ship could traverse. He found it unbelievable that they had once been the "markets of the Mediterranean" and the very forefront of civilization.

Antonio awoke from his daydreams of the ancient world to realize that Orsini had at some point returned and now was looking at him through one of the grille windows around the bridge. The young Roman knight's eyes, filled with an amused irony, seemed capable of reading his comrade's thoughts. Antonio, Orsini's junior by five years, was somewhat disappointed that there was again something that he couldn't share. Orsini seemed to detect that sentiment in Antonio's face and immediately tried to dispel it.

"You know, the island of Kas might be called the prison of the Knights of St. John. Those who commit a crime or break the rules of the order are exiled there. There's no jail, but service on such a tiny, desolate island is punishment in itself. I was sent there once. Though I didn't show much remorse, the Grand Master gave up and recalled me before half a year had passed. The men there now are not the type to follow rules…a merry bunch, indeed."

Antonio laughed despite himself, but he knew that the real reason Orsini had been recalled to Rhodes, despite his lack of remorse, was not that the Grand Master had given up. The pope at that time, Leo X, had been mothered by a Giambattista, which made Orsini his relative. Cardinal Giulio, like the pope a Medici, was a knight in the Order of St. John. Although Giulio had neither spent time in a monastery nor crossed swords with Muslims, his letter on Orsini's behalf, which conveyed the pope's wishes in the matter, was not something the Grand Master could ignore. Thus Orsini only served six months of his sentenced year in exile.

Orsini was more than just a maverick, however. He also possessed great talent that sooner or later had to be recognized. This was especially the case in the Order of the Knights of St. John, which constantly had to be ready for war. Chances for recognition and promotion came sooner and more often than they would have in times of peace. Orsini's appointment as the leader of these inspections was a case in point.

Kas bordered the southern coast of Asia Minor so closely that it seemed impossible for the knights to get any closer to enemy territory. Perhaps no more than five kilometers separated it from the mainland. From one of the handful of posts on the island, one could see the lights on the opposite shore clearly enough to count them.

Orsini had come with orders from the Grand Master for everyone to abandon the island. The so-called enemy on the facing shore consisted of nothing but a few villages. Even if their charge was to maintain control of the seas, there was no point in keeping twenty knights here other than to punish them. There had been no recent sign of Turkish ships, and the knights had grown weary from idleness. They were thrilled to be returning to Rhodes and quickly completed preparations for departure. This concluded the inspections. All that remained now was to go back to Rhodes.

The galley's prow once again turned west as they left the island. The Ponente, or western wind, however, was strong. While their ship may have been known for its speed, it was certainly not fast now, and in fact could only make progress by tacking left and right. Under such conditions, the positions of the triangular sails unfurled on the three masts had to be constantly adjusted, so the sailors were busy and the captain didn't have a moment's rest on the bridge. Antonio and Orsini therefore had plenty of time to speak in private.

A Disappearing Class

Antonio del Carretto and Giambattista Orsini could be described as related albeit very distantly. The Orsinis were related to the Medicis, and a Medici daughter, Maddalena, had married Franceschetto Cibo, nephew of Innocent VIII, the pope four reigns prior. Maddalena's father was none other than Lorenzo the Magnificent, *de facto* king of the Republic of Florence; she was also the younger sister of Leo X, the previous pope.

In addition to Franceschetto, Pope Innocent VIII also had a niece, Teodorina, who married a wealthy Genoese named Uso di Mare. Antonio's mother Peretta was one of the children of that union, and she married Alfonso del Carretto. Orsini and Antonio were thus related through the Medicis and Cibos, two of the reigning families of late-fifteenth-century Italy.

Yet for some reason Orsini roared with laughter for a long time when Antonio explained this to him.

"If that counts as 'being related,'" he said, "then the Orsinis are related to every family that's the least bit famous."

Antonio seemed hurt. As if to console him, Orsini added, "Do you think that the strategy that our families have employed of creating alliances through marriage matters anymore? I don't think so. Until now, creating a network of relations aided in safeguarding our families' independence. Things will be different. Alliance by marriage will continue, but only to help our houses maintain whatever tenuous existence we can under the reigns of powerful monarchs. Didn't a del Carretto become a marquis just recently?"

"Yes, my father Alfonso was granted the title of marquis by the Holy Roman Emperor Maximilian I," said Antonio.

"A number of branches of the Orsini family have become counts and marquises," Orsini explained, "but the main family is simply called baron or *signore* (master). We have not yet been annexed into the ranks of court nobles, but it's only a matter of time." (Indeed, thirty-eight years later, the main Orsini family is granted the rank of duke.)

Antonio knew the history of the tremendously powerful Orsini family. If one were to count the most famous families in Italy, the Orsinis would not only be in the top five, they would be in competition for first. The del Carrettos didn't even come close. The two representative families of Rome after the twelfth century were the Colonnas and the Orsinis. The Colonna family held territory to the south of Rome. The Orsini family was based in the area that spread north of the city. The two families were famous for their repeated clashes. In the thirteenth century, when the Guelphs (papal faction) and the Ghibellines (imperial faction) locked horns, the Orsini family joined the Guelphs and the Colonna family joined the Ghibellines, perpetuating their antagonism. For successive popes, coping with these two powerful families, which had themselves produced popes, was always a top concern. As both of these families had traditionally been passionate about creating marriage alliances with influential families throughout Europe, foreign popes or those from unknown families agonized over how to deal with them.

The Medicis were originally merchants, but when they decided to seek status in addition to wealth, they married their eldest son to an Orsini. This decision was motivated by the fact that there had never been a time when an Orsini or Colonna wasn't serving as a cardinal in the Vatican. Thus, even when the pope was not one of their relations, both families always had potential papal candidates. In order to benefit from the special authority of the pope, royal and noble houses welcomed associations with these two families. The only exception was the Venetian aristocracy, who had decided to protect their sovereignty by eschewing intermarriage with the notable families of other states.

While it was impossible to judge which of the two Roman families was more successful at forging ties with the Vatican and the dominant houses of Europe, the Orsinis were clearly far better at establishing themselves in the knightly orders.

Around the time the Orsini family began sending its men to the Order of the Knights of St. John, the Colonna family grew close to the Knights Templar. When the Knights Templar disappeared at the beginning of the fourteenth century, the Colonna family's ambitions were shattered. From then on, Hospitaller St. John was the only knightly religious order, one in which the Orsinis had established deep roots. An Orsini even became Grand Master in the latter half of the fifteenth century.

The Orsinis' efforts to infiltrate all the corridors of power didn't end there. Many of the family's men made inroads into the armies of Italy and other Western European countries by serving as mercenaries. Yet, because it was customary in the mercenary system of the time to contract hired commanders who had their own contingents, the Orsinis who did this were typically from branches of the family that had their own small territories and were partially independent. Most of them no longer went by the name Orsini and instead assumed the names of their domains, like the Count of Trulli or the Count of Petriano. There would be clear political ramifications if the head of the main house became a mercenary commander, since the entire clan would then be linked to the Vatican, the King of Naples, or whomever its employer might be. On the contrary, the branches of the family enjoyed great freedom in forming and breaking contracts. For the employers, this was quite convenient. For the employed, this had certain merits, too. The mercenary trade was a profitable business throughout that era. The Colonna family also used the profession as an avenue to power—yet another arena in which the two families were rivals.

Even the tremendously powerful Orsini family suffered an era of decline, however, when Alessandro VI, a man determined to augment the power of his office, became pope. While the Orsini and the Colonna families controlled vast territories, those territories were located within the provinces of the Papal State. Alessandro VI, who came from the Borgia family, decided that the only way to strengthen papal authority was to sweep away any family powerful enough to exercise its will unhindered. He placed his son Cesare in a position to accomplish just that. The families were doubly unlucky—Cesare was no ordinary young man. The Orsinis came within inches of extinction when two of their key men were sentenced to death and the Orsini cardinals were forced to serve prison terms. Giambattista himself, though he eventually became a knight on Rhodes, spent his first years in exile. He had been born just as the Borgian army surrounded his natal castle.

In 1503, however, the sudden collapse of the Borgias gave the Orsinis a new lease on life. They managed to reestablish their links and influence in the Vatican through the marriage of one of their own to the daughter of the next pope, Giulio II. The pope after that, Leo X, was the child of Clarice Orsini, who had married into the Medici family.

This was all public knowledge, familiar even to someone like Antonio, who had been born in a coastal castle near Genoa. He found Giambattista's perennial air of melancholy unjustified given that he was a direct descendant of the Orsini family, on which the sun never seemed to set. When Antonio said as much, the young Roman knight laughed. As if speaking to a younger brother, he patiently explained:

"The noble families of Venice and Florence, who make up the ruling class, are a special case. They are called nobles, but have no titles. The nobility, whose power is centered on land holdings, is divided into dukes, marquises, counts, and barons. The sources of these titles were the Byzantine Emperor and the monarchs of other European countries, who all rose to power after the fall of the Roman Empire.

"Dukes, originally pronounced *dux* in Latin and later *duca* in Italian, were the chief bureaucrats of the emperors and kings. They were essentially regional administrators in charge of the governmental and military affairs in their provinces. 'Count' was the name given to those who did the same job in Frankish lands, although they were responsible for smaller territories. The administrators of peripheral regions were called marquises, or *marche*, which means guard of the border.

"Considering these etymological roots, only the title baron, or *barone*, which means 'free man,' does not imply being the subject of an emperor or king. Barons had their own territory, collected taxes, dispensed justice, and some even had the right to mint currency. These barons only had to give a portion of the taxes they collected to the ruler of the larger domain, the emperor, king, or lord.

"There were many counts and marquises in the northern and central swaths of Italy, which were controlled by the Longobardo family; barons, however, ruled in the south. You del Carrettos are marquises, while we Orsinis are barons. But in the distant branches of my family, there are many counts. In both northern and southern Italy, the barons maintained a status quite different from that of the court nobles until the fourteenth century. While the lords were poor, the barons, who supposedly ranked beneath them, were rich.

"Although the sovereign could summon the barons in his domain when he wanted to go to war, he could not order them to fight. That was always something decided by personal agreement. If the sovereign violated their contract, the baron not only had the right to leave the battlefield but could even turn and fight against the sovereign. This state of affairs continued in southern Italy for quite some time, even after the fourteenth century. There the highest organ of power was the conference of barons that convened twice a year. The Principe, who served as the chairman, was neither preeminent nor more powerful than the rest; he was merely a first among equals. We have records of the oaths that barons of that time made to their sovereigns, and they are quite hilarious:

> Each and every one of us barons is as worthy as you, and when we assemble together we are worthier than you. Though we pledge our loyalty, it is contingent upon whether or not you respect our inherited rights and privileges. If you are negligent in this regard, our oath of fidelity will be rendered null and void.

"All the barons would loudly chant this oath in front of the sovereign. Feudal lords certainly didn't have it easy! To the sovereigns, who strove to establish strong centralized control, it must have seemed like anarchy.

"Little by little, the movement to stifle the barons' power gained momentum, but the barons caught on and further entrenched themselves. The conflict finally boiled over with the famous 'Rebellion of the Barons' in 1460, the war between King Ferrante of Naples and the barons in his territory. Ferrante won. One branch of the Orsini family took part in that struggle and suffered a major setback. We no longer live in a world where we can chant hilarious oaths. The wave of centralization is inescapable no matter where you are.

"Only in Rome are things somewhat different. While the rulers of other nations can bequeath their positions to their heirs, the pope cannot. In Rome, the ruler changes while the barons stay.

"Yet, even if the grand Orsini and Colonna families are able to maintain our power in and around Rome thanks to fortuitous circumstances, what would be the point? The Colonnas are practically the subjects of Charles, which is only natural since a mercenary cannot serve a sovereign without becoming his subject. My family won't be able to resist this wave of centralization, either. We will become the subjects of some ruler who gives us titles in return for making us protect a tiny territory that only belongs to us in name. The barons, or free men, will disappear and the Orsini name will survive only by being assigned a place in the court nobility.

"Likewise, knights are being replaced by infantrymen. The appearance of the cannon has altered the nature of combat. Barons once gained the respect of the people and the right to command territory by protecting the populace from outside enemies. Having ceded that role to the sovereign, barons can no longer act like masters. You and I are both knights of the Order of St. John, which only accepts those of noble blood, and we are moreover both nobility who are losing seigniorial rights. Ours is a particular misfortune—being the last of a disappearing class.

"Isn't it ironic that we are to fight the Turks, whose army rose to greatness through the use of cannons and human waves? A class that is dying out is always forced to perish battling the class that is replacing it."

Antonio felt he had been forced to face reality. The del Carretto family, while not as powerful as the Orsinis, had for four hundred years been the lords of the territory they had won for themselves in Savoia, near Genoa. Yet, for the last hundred years, they had no longer been able to remain indifferent to the battles raging among the great powers that surrounded them. At times they drew close to the Sforza rulers of the Dukedom of Milan, and at other times they formed alliances with the Republic of Genoa. Then, thirty years ago, they were forced either to clarify their loyalties or face extinction. It was then that Antonio's father, Alfonso, became a subject of the German Holy Roman Emperor and given the title of marquis. At that moment Antonio suddenly envied the French knight La Vallete, in whose unflinching gaze he failed to detect even a moment's hesitation regarding the order's reason for existence or his nobility.

The oarsmen of Antonio and Orsini's galley acquired new vigor as they neared the final leg of their voyage. The Isle of Rhodes, which appeared on the western horizon, rapidly seemed to grow larger. When Antonio finally saw the remains of the Lindos Acropolis about which he had heard so much, the boat's prow was suddenly turned to the north. It was standard practice for ships coming from the east to follow this route along the island's coast to the capital. Under the ancient Greek pillars shining white atop Lindos hill sat a fort, one of the order's. It occurred to Antonio that he may never serve there.

Just before entering the port of the city of Rhodes, the ship changed course again. Smoke could be seen rising from the far side of town. A large area must have been burning, because the smoke covered half the sky. Antonio was wondering what had happened when Orsini's words allowed him to breathe a sigh of relief. Orsini told him that in preparation for the enemy's attack, the order was burning the fields, crops, and even the houses outside of the walls. They had to strip the land of every tree in the entire area where the enemy was expected to camp.

"The skylarks must be rattled about the loss of their nests," Orsini remarked.

Antonio smiled at these words. It was now June. Battles normally took place from spring to autumn. No doubt the Grand Master had received word of an unmistakable move by the Turkish Army.

Chapter Five

Summer 1522

The Approaching Clouds of War

Even the Genoese and Venetian merchants, whom the order often criticized for placing commerce above all else, had to realize in the end that they had to support their coreligionists when faced with such a clear confrontation between Islam and Christianity. They were still conscious of their Catholicism, which in turn never let them forget that they were in fact Western Europeans. A similar change of heart, though, could not be expected from fellow Christians such as the Greeks or Armenians, who followed the Greek Orthodox faith. Protestant indifference also remained unchanged. German and Dutch merchants, for their part, had yet to venture into the Mediterranean. Therefore, if anyone were to provide information to the order, it had to be Catholic traders from Western Europe.

These always carried out trade with no regard to differences of religion. Halting their shipping whenever war clouds loomed over the Eastern Mediterranean would mean the end of business. As long as their own country wasn't at war, it wasn't considered strange for their ships to call on Turkish ports and for their local representatives at branch offices to conduct business as usual. Thus, even though the Order of the Knights of St. John had never maintained an independent, high-level institution with the capacity to collect information, it never lacked intelligence whenever clashes with the Turks seemed imminent. This was one of the benefits of being a religious order. They didn't need to dispatch their own spies since they could use Western European merchants to obtain extremely detailed information on the scale and movements of the Turkish forces.

The Turkish fleet was intent on capturing Rhodes and assembled in the waters off of Constantinople (Istanbul), the capital of the Ottoman Empire, on the first of June 1522. One account numbered the ships at seven hundred, but the Western European merchants reported just over three hundred. Based upon the scale of traditional Turkish fleets, three hundred seems the more probable figure.

The pirate captain Kurtoglu commanded the fleet. The Turks had no tradition of trade and their navy was not particularly organized, so a pirate captain was commonly installed as the commander when the time came for serious warfare. Kurtoglu loaded the three hundred ships with ten thousand soldiers and set out for the Dardanelles Strait through the Marmara Sea. Relatively few men were aboard each ship because the fleet's primary objective was to transport cannons and other weapons of siege warfare.

The army on the Asian side of the Strait of Bosphorus finished assembling at around the same time. It numbered 100,000 strong; a corps of miners conscripted from the Greek Orthodox population in the Turkish-controlled Balkans was particularly conspicuous. The sultan joined the column of soldiers leaving the European continent and was accompanied by all of his viziers (who were addressed by the title "pasha"), demonstrating the Ottoman court's unanimous support for the war effort.

This, however, was not the sum of the invading forces. Two hundred ships bearing 100,000 soldiers were to be sent from Syria and Egypt, which had been conquered by the Turks five years earlier. The army was twice as large as the one that took part in the campaign against Rhodes forty years earlier. A mobilization of such overwhelming scale to attack Rhodes, which was pea-sized in comparison to the vast Ottoman Empire, gives a sense of the twenty-eight-year old Sultan Suleiman's enthusiasm for the battle. It was necessary, in order to preserve the honor of the great Ottoman Empire, to eradicate this "nest of Christian vipers" once and for all.

The fleet left Constantinople on June 1st and, after passing through the Dardanelles, stopped briefly at the island of Lesbos to replenish its supplies. In the seas from there to Rhodes, the Turks and their great fleet could only expect to put into port at Smyrna. The island of Chios sat in the waters near Smyrna; although declared neutral, it was in fact a possession of Genoa. A mere ten kilometers separated Chios from Asia Minor. Three hundred Turkish ships passing through all at once virtually plugged up the entire strait. All activity on Chios came to a halt as the Turkish ships passed.

Past this strait were the territorial waters of the Order of the Knights of St. John. The Turks, however, were well aware of the paucity of military strength on the order's outlying islands. Although the Turks were at a disadvantage in one-on-one naval combat, a fleet of three hundred ships was a different matter. Perhaps as a way to flex their muscles, Kurtoglu decided to try to capture the island of Kos, something which was not a part of the sultan's strategy. The knights garrisoned in the fortress, however, fought back fiercely. Realizing this would not be an easy conquest, Kurtoglu quickly lifted the siege and the fleet resumed its southbound course. On June 26th, ships from the vanguard of the Turkish fleet made their first appearance in the waters off Rhodes.

The main force of soldiers, who had left at the same time as the fleet and were traveling across Asia Minor, arrived at the port of Marmaris in less than a month. Their voyage along the western coast was through their own territory, so there was no need to worry about conflicts with locals along the way. They completely bypassed Bodrum, which was located at the tip of a peninsula off the main route. It would have been a waste of time and manpower to attack the Knights there. If Rhodes fell, then Kos and Bodrum would follow suit. The sultan's presence ensured his strategy would be carried out to the letter, and the 100,000-man army successfully reassembled, almost fully unharmed, at the port of Marmaris. Once the fleet deposited its cannons, weapons, and gunpowder on Rhodes, it would return to Marmaris to fetch the army.

The Knights of St. John were in no mood to squander resources, either. The Turkish fleet approached Rhodes from the northwest, bypassed the mouth of the harbor, and circumnavigated the island to a sandy beach approximately five kilometers south. As the Turks disembarked their numerous cannons and siege weapons, the knights made no effort to stop them. The enemy, including the sailors, numbered ten thousand. The men defending the fortress city of Rhodes consisted of fewer than six hundred knights, approximately fifteen hundred mercenaries, and three thousand able-bodied Rhodians. This was all they could hope for. They couldn't afford to waste a single soldier.

Thus the Knights offered no opposition even after the Turkish fleet had successfully unloaded their weapons, tents, and perishable provisions and began the process of going back and forth between Marmaris and Rhodes to transport the main army. Three hundred ships is, to say the least, a large force. If the order hoped to avoid a naval blockade, they had to make sure not to lose a single one of their own ships. For the whole month of July, while the northwesterly winds intensified, the residents of Rhodes labored to strengthen the defenses that would face the inevitable siege. During that time, they watched the comings and goings of the Turkish ships—loaded with soldiers—passing in the seas just outside of the booms made of iron chains as thick as a man's arm that sealed off the entrances to both the military and merchant harbors.

This was to be Antonio's first experience defending a fortress, and his first time fighting against the Turks. He was surprised that the population of the island seemed to have doubled. Although that wasn't exactly the case, it appeared that way because far more people were out on the streets and in the square. That being said, the number of people in the city had indeed increased to the extent that those living outside the city walls, whose homes and fields had been torched, were now taking refuge inside them. They had brought their livestock, sheep, chicken and even dogs with them when they sought safety in the city. The resulting din from the residential district in the southern part of town was as loud as that of a market festival.

Watching barefooted children chasing the dogs and chickens, Antonio could hardly believe that a siege was imminent. The commotion had not reached the northern half of the city, where the order's buildings were concentrated, but it was common practice for the gates in the thin wall that separated the knights' district from that of the commoners to be left open during the daytime. Occasionally a sheep would stray in with a shabbily dressed child chasing after it. Antonio couldn't but smile at the wide-eyed curiosity of these children as they watched the knights come and go. They were about to be attacked by a massive infidel army but the people of the city went about their lives as always. Whenever Antonio began to worry that his own life might soon come to an end at the age of twenty, these scenes came back to rescue him. When not on duty, he frequently visited a church in the commoners' district, but not to pray; these churches, both Catholic and Greek Orthodox, were being used to provide temporary shelter for the refugee farmers.

At night, however, the atmosphere grew tense. All gates separating the two halves of the city were closed.

Torches burned brightly in front of the knights' residences, the hospital, the armory, and also the Grand Master's Palace, so that any suspicious persons could be spotted, even among the shadows. In the commoners' section of the city, where a curfew had been issued, there was nothing to light the pitch-black streets other than the torches that burned all night and that illuminated the sacred statues placed within the niches of buildings. The streets were periodically traversed by patrols of approximately twenty soldiers. For one score nights already, an order had been in effect for all shops to close at sunset, including the taverns that normally burned their torches well into the night.

The Grand Master had yet to receive any good news from the envoys he had sent out six months earlier requesting assistance; he decided to dispatch even more envoys throughout Western Europe. He sent Spanish knights to the pope and to Emperor Charles, and French knights to the French king. Another pair of knights set out on a journey to round up the knights of the order scattered throughout Western Europe. They carried news of the danger faced by the home base as well as a general mobilization order. They were given the additional task of procuring as much gunpowder and as many provisions as possible to ship back to Rhodes. The knights so designated left in lightweight fast galleys, each with a different destination. They slipped out of the harbor in the middle of the night and none was stopped by the Turks.

In the summer of 1522, however, Western Europe had

other things to worry about. The pope-to-be was sailing through the western Mediterranean, heading for his coronation at St. Peter's Basilica in Rome. Dubbed Adrian VI, he had been selected on January 9th of that year, but only left Spain on July 8th. His ship docked in the harbor of Genoa on July 17th, and then arrived in Ostia, the port city of Rome, on August 28th. The coronation ceremony followed on August 31st. At the very least, he had managed to make it to Rome without accepting any of the "favors" offered by Emperor Charles, King François I of France, or the English King Henry VIII, and without causing them any offense.

Because of this delay, the pope couldn't deliver his inaugural declaration of Church policy at the College of Cardinals until September. Adrian VI was expected to engage two issues only: facilitating cooperation among Christians in resisting the Turks and addressing the Protestant movement, active primarily in Germany. The new pope clearly intended to enlist all the ruling princes of Europe in the effort to resolve these two major problems facing the Christian world. The princes, for their part, only cared about waging war amongst themselves.

Charles ruled Germany and the Netherlands as the Holy Roman Emperor. As the king of Spain, he also controlled Spain and the New World. He and King François I of France were also in contention for Italy. A battle near Milan in April of that year, however, decisively determined Charles's superiority. The French king abandoned Milan, and rule over Genoa transferred from France to Spain. Since Spain had previously acquired

Naples and Sicily in southern Italy, the traditional feud between France and Spain over Italy was, at least for the time being, settled in Spain's favor.

In addition, the King of England, Henry VIII, had formed an alliance with Charles in June. In July an English army commanded by the Duke of Suffolk landed in Normandy. It was unthinkable that France, ruled by a sage king and possessing the most fertile farmland in Europe, would easily yield to the Hapsburgs, but she was on the defensive.

The envoys from the Order of Knights of St. John, who were charged with reporting the arrival of the Turkish expedition and requesting assistance, reached Europe only to find a situation of utter disarray. All the rulers of Europe recognized the order as the "last stronghold of Christianity in the Eastern Mediterranean," but in every age the link between thought and deed is tenuous at best.

With the arrival on Rhodes of Sultan Suleiman I on July 28th, the attacking Turkish army was finally complete.

A Throng of Tents

The Turkish force of 100,000 was divided into six corps, each assuming a distinct formation. Since the position of the troops had been decided in advance, their movements, when viewed from atop the city walls, seemed quite orderly for an army of 100,000 men.

The corps led by Piri Pasha spread its formation on the nearly level ground along the moat in front of the Italian section of the fortress wall. In front of the fortifications entrusted to the knights from Provence, Kazim Pasha's troops arrayed their tents. Mustafa Pasha's soldiers made their encampment on the level ground opposite the rampart protected by the English knights, while those of Ahmed Pasha were dug in across the moat and wall defended by the knights from Aragon. Ayas Pasha's troops were reserves; though encamped facing the German rampart, their tents were pitched relatively far from the moat. Agla Pasha led the 15,000-man corps of Janissaries facing the fortifications protected by the knights from Auvergne, while the sultan's tent was raised on the hill facing Aragon's fortress wall, since it was the highest spot in the area. The Janissaries, who were the sultan's personal bodyguard, always based themselves nearby in order to be ready for anything.

This battle formation was a clear indication to the defenders just which parts of the fortress would bear the brunt of the attack. The main assaults would be led by the four viziers and directed against the ramparts defended by Italy, Provence, England and Aragon—exactly as Grand Master Fabrizio del Carretto had predicted eight years earlier. He had aggressively reinforced precisely those parts of the fortress wall, so that they now presented a formidable obstacle to the Turks' offensive. The problem was that, although great strides had been made in fortress-wall construction in the seventy years since the fall of Constantinople, the techniques for attacking those walls had not exactly stood still, either.

The splendor of the sultan's tent put all the others to shame. It also far exceeded anything a European might have had in mind when he thought of a "tent." Every inch glimmered with such a golden sheen that there appeared to be not just one, but several layers of gold folded on top of one another. The interior was divided into several chambers and, with all manner of amenities being carried in by the soldiers, must have rivaled the comfort of Topkapi Palace. The only thing lacking: a harem of three hundred beautiful girls languishing in a garden lush with tulips. The Turks believed that any battle against infidels was a holy war performed as a service to Allah and would never bring a woman to the battlefield. Suleiman's magnificent tent could be seen from any part of Rhodes's fortress wall.

Though inferior to that of the sultan, the tents of the viziers were also conspicuous in their extravagance.

It must have been lavish golden embroidery on its field of green that covered Piri Pasha's tent, located in front of the Italian rampart, for it gave the gorgeous appearance of satin damask. In front of Provence's wall, the tent of Kazim Pasha had, on a background of blue, silver embroidery that marvelously reflected the sunlight. Then there was Mustafa Pasha's tent, which faced the English rampart. His marriage to the sultan's younger sister and subsequent elevation of status afforded him a tent with golden embroidery blanketing a background of red. Ahmed Pasha's tent, in front of the rampart of Aragon, had silver and purple embroidery on a sky-blue background. It was behind these, high on the hill, that the sultan's golden tent sat adorned with a golden crescent moon on its peak.

The tents of the battalion commanders were also bedecked with lovely colors, though they never had gold or silver embroidery. The soldiers' tents were earth-colored and filled the spaces between the occasional splashes of beautiful hues. Enemy tents covered the landscape as far as the eye could see when viewed from the tower of the Grand Master's Palace in the highest part of the city. The immense size of the 100,000-man enemy was for the first time a shocking reality and weighed heavily on the hearts of the knights.

They spent the last days of July watching the enemy position mortars and cannons on the far banks of the moat. The mortars were shaped like rounded bowls and had gigantic muzzles tilted slightly upward. The cannons had impressively long barrels and muzzles that, although slightly smaller, pointed directly at the knights. The sheer weight of these weapons made it difficult to build the platforms on which they needed to be mounted. The Turkish soldiers performed their work in silence, completely ignoring the knights. The distance between the fortress walls and the opposite embankment where the Turks were at work came at some points to forty meters, which was beyond the effective range of small firearms and arrows. Although the knights had placed cannons in their forts, the Turks were not foolish enough to work in the line of their fire.

At sunset on the last day before August, an arrow carrying a letter bearing the sultan's seal was shot into the English Fort. The letter was immediately taken to Grand Master L'Isle-Adam, who invited all the knights to the gardens of his residence that evening. The Grand Master himself read the sultan's letter aloud. It said: "Despite having urged you three times to surrender, I have yet to receive a sensible reply. I, Sultan Suleiman, will therefore commence hostilities at sunrise tomorrow."

When he had finished reading, the Grand Master said, "We will once again greet the enemy in a manner appropriate to the Order of the Knights of St. John." This meant that every member, dressed head to toe in full armor, would line up along the ramparts in the morning and await the enemy. Suleiman, too, enjoyed conspicuous displays of propriety and etiquette and resembled in this way the noblemen of the order. Both exhibited a chivalrous spirit when it was convenient to do so and promptly dispensed with it when it was not.

The Siege Begins

On August 1st the first shots were fired in the siege of Rhodes, just as the sultan had warned. The opening salvo, more a test firing of the cannons than anything else, came at the Italian rampart and continued in stages to the Provençal, English, and Aragonese sections. On the defensive side, six hundred knights arrayed atop the walls greeted the enemy in full armor, shining silver in the morning sun. Each knight's armor was slightly different: its splendor was an index of his family's relative wealth. What they all had in common, however, were the white crosses on fields of red adorning their breastplates and capes. The tips of their lances reflected the sun. Every unit flew its own colors. Grand Master L'Isle-Adam stood unmoving atop the Aragonese rampart like a guardian deity, enveloped in the smoke of the cannonade, while the battle flag of the Order of the Knights of St. John flew behind him as if in counterpoint to the sultan's tent.

This spectacle seemed to sap some of the Turkish soldiers' courage. Encased from head to toe in steel armor, a knight exerted greater psychological pressure on his opponent than an ordinary warrior. The entire order, lined up thus atop the walls, seemed to the Turkish soldiers to be something more than a mere six hundred men.

Armored knights were the very embodiment of the Middle Ages, but they could only exert their full power and mobility on battlegrounds that afforded movement on horseback. They were only half as effective when fighting on foot from atop a wall. The impact of their demonstration, however, was a different matter altogether. It certainly couldn't have been easy for these brave knights to stand strong and unflinching in the midst of the smoke and falling cannon fire, but the Turkish artillerymen were not yet familiar with the lay of the land, so the barrage ended with virtually no casualties. All it had done was create a lot of smoke.

The improvements in the walls of Rhodes had entailed, rather than higher walls, deeper and thicker ones. Thus, defenders and attackers on either side of the deep, wide moat were situated at virtually identical elevations. The defenders were slightly higher by a difference that had been carefully calculated.

The walls' outer edge was at the same elevation as the embankment, but they gradually increased in height toward the interior. Seen from the side, the walls formed a gentle slope. This reduced by nearly half the impact of a direct hit from a cannonball. Both the main fortress wall and the outer fortress wall facing the enemy sloped gently toward the base.

Whether fired from mortars or cannons, rounded stones were the artillery shots of the time, and they did not explode upon impact. The force of the impact was what inflicted damage, and the stronger the impact, the greater the damage. If defenders could lessen the impact of the direct hits they were no longer at the mercy of cannons.

Additionally, in the case of Rhodes, layers of soft earth covered places where the cannonballs were likely to land, such as in the moat or just inside of the walls. No matter the angle at which they landed, the heavy stone balls would simply burrow into the ground. There would be no flying debris, just a cloud of dust.

If the target were built very high and extended for a great distance like the walls of Constantinople, an artilleryman who knew the range to it could usually score a sound hit. In Rhodes, however, where the heavy firearms were at nearly the same elevation as their target, the only damage that could be expected was from the weight of the shot itself. This served to lessen the initial fears the defenders might have had of the vaunted Turkish artillery. The commoners, mercenaries, and knights, in that order, experienced a surge in morale. The city was so lively it seemed possible to forget that it was under siege, and even the children began to believe they could outlast the threat.

An incident several days later only added to their high spirits. The Turkish fleet under Kurtoglu was responsible for maintaining a maritime blockade, yet its attempt to capture the Fort of St. Nicholas, which towered between the naval and merchant harbors, ended in dismal failure. The fort had been the Turks' main target forty years earlier; this time the locus of battle was on land, with the navy's only task being the blockade. As long as the fort continued to act as a stronghold, however, a complete blockade of both harbors was impossible. Whenever the twenty-five French knights and fifty soldiers defending the fort saw a Turkish ship approach, fire would belch forth from their cannons. The Turks' small, wooden ships disintegrated under a direct hit. With no maritime tradition to speak of, the Turks were making do with boats of poor construction.

Even when they were able to avoid direct cannon hits,

they still had to worry about flaming arrows fired from the defenders' crossbows. Turkish sailors had yet to master the technique of circling their ships out of range in a ring—nor could they drop anchor, since the water was relatively deep out of port. Furthermore, the northwesterly Mistral blew especially hard during the summer. The slightest bit of carelessness caused the Turks to be blown towards one of Rhodes's two harbors. In fact, pilot error caused one Turkish merchant ship to crash into the harbor boom and get captured. The knights who boarded that ship interrogated its crew and were able to extract valuable information.

Though the Turkish fleet failed in their blockade despite counting three hundred ships, they were not exactly wasting their time. Most of the vessels were making nearly daily runs between Rhodes and Marmaris. They were busy bringing supplies to the 100,000-man encampment so that the troops could remain focused on the offensive. While the rations provided by the Turkish army were infamously bad, just keeping 100,000 mouths full was a feat in itself. The residents of Rhodes found it necessary to import wheat even during peacetime because of the island's low production. Sheep were the predominant livestock, yet the herders had taken refuge in the city. Those in remote regions had been given advance warning by the order and had fled to rugged mountain terrain by the time the Turks arrived. In addition, all the nearby wells and springs had been filled in so that the enemy could not use them for water. The Turkish army had no choice but to ship in all supplies.

Suleiman, however, seemed to have anticipated this in formulating his strategy. If the Turkish ships could make it to Marmaris, everything from water, flour, mutton, and even the gunpowder and cannonballs used by the artillery, were waiting there to be loaded. Thinning supplies were replenished in no time at all. Asia Minor was well known for its wheat production.

Suleiman chose to shuttle his boats fifty kilometers over the sea rather than disperse his soldiers throughout the mountains of Rhodes in order to acquire water and wheat. Although there was a headwind on the way to Marmaris, the ships making that passage were not weighed down. Tailwinds on the return voyage to Rhodes made the trip easy even for those ships loaded with cannonballs. The twenty-eight-year-old sultan exercised sound judgment in choosing to send all supplies from his own territory instead of expecting farmers of an enemy land to obey and supply goods under duress.

The leaders of the order hadn't foreseen this approach. They expected the Turks to procure their provisions from within Rhodes as they had in 1480. Based on that precedent, the knights envisioned that holding off the Turks long enough would plunge them into critical supply shortages once again. As the quality of their provisions deteriorated and water became scarce, diseases would break out and the enemy would have no choice but to give up the siege and withdraw. But given Suleiman's strategy, that was no longer a possibility. On the contrary, it was the defenders who would suffer the longer the siege drew out.

The knights hastily called a council meeting to discuss a strategy for cutting off the Turkish supply route. The leaders of the English and Italian delegations proposed to send out warships from the order's fleet to attack Turkish ships en route to Marmaris, when they would be contending with the headwind. The navy of the order had traditionally been entrusted to knights hailing from those two countries.

Information gathered by reconnaissance ships, however, dashed any such hopes. It seemed the Turks had anticipated this counterstrategy and were traveling in convoys of about twenty ships. The knights realized their plan would be unsuccessful unless they mobilized all of their ships, including those at the bases at Kos and Bodrum.

The English and Italian knights were nonetheless adamant about going through with it. The knights from the French delegations were opposed; Ile-de-France, Provence and Auvergne all categorically rejected any strategy that would abandon Kos or Bodrum. The French passion for acquiring territory and abhorrence for abandoning it was apparently something that held sway over the Frenchmen in the Order of St. John as well.

The Turkish supply route therefore continued to function without any interdiction. At the very least, however, the order was able to take pride in the fact that it was able to remain in contact with its bases on Kos and Bodrum, and even with Lindos on Rhodes, despite having to contend with three hundred heathen ships.

Strength in Numbers

Sultan Suleiman wasn't discouraged by the ineffec-
tiveness of the Turkish cannonade. He believed that the
initial offensive in August had failed to bring substantial
results because the cannons had been situated slightly
lower than the defenders. The work of building elevated
platforms for these cannons had already begun. These
wooden platforms not only had to hold the weight of the
cannons, but also withstand the force of their recoil. The
Turks were unwilling to halt their attacks while a large
number of these platforms were built, so for several days
they turned their attention to the German and Auvergne
ramparts, which had yet to be pelted.

These walls had hardly been touched by Fabrizio del
Carretto's reconstruction efforts. The fortress walls were
very high, so the casemates were too narrow for cannons.
Still, the depth and width of the moat was the same as
everywhere else, so the barrage here hardly caused more
devastation than elsewhere. One cannonball, however,
struck dead center and partially broke through the wall
before coming to a halt.

The artillery platforms were completed in the middle of August. When the defenders looked out, they saw
an evenly elevated line of enemy cannons. Midsummer in
Rhodes brought northwesterly winds from the sea, which
blew over the city quarters and into the Turkish army's
camps. Although the defenders had destroyed all the
trees and homes in the outside grounds so that nothing

remained to provide the Turks with shade, the latter only had soil underfoot. Had the grounds been rocky, they would have had to contend with the reflected heat of the hot summer sun. Even when the temperatures reached the high eighties, constant breezes from the sea eased the toil of continuing under the midsummer glare.

Even after elevating their cannons, the Turks were unable to increase their number of good hits by any significant measure. Suleiman decided to make up for this simply by firing off more rounds. No matter how many cannonballs and how much gunpowder they used, their supply was always replenished, so this was not a problem. Naturally, the more rounds they fired, the more hits they scored. The destruction first became noticeable in the outer wall of the English section. Nonetheless the Turkish army couldn't launch an assault until they were able to cross the moat. Thus far, the fatalities suffered by the defenders had been limited to one knight and a small number of mercenaries— men who had been killed defending the outer wall of the English Fort. The loss had not dampened the defenders' fighting spirit. Quite the contrary.

On the last day of August, a single ship sailed into the harbor of Rhodes, flouting the Turkish blockade. The ship had come from Naples. Though it bore only four knights and a handful of mercenaries, it was also packed with gunpowder. The ship had been outfitted and dispatched by an Italian branch of the Order of the Knights of St. John, and its arrival supplied the defenders with a satisfaction far out of proportion to the men and supplies it carried. The ship's successful arrival proved that the Turks' blockade was ineffective, and it also gave hope that Western Europe had not abandoned the Isle of Rhodes. The sultan, on the other hand, was furious. Upon hearing the news, he had Kurtoglu tied to a ship's mast and whipped until his naked body was covered with rivulets of blood.

Autumn

The Turkish reliance on overwhelming numbers and supplies eventually began to bear fruit in September. The defenders had anticipated attacks from both cannons above ground and mines below, and so it came to pass.

The term "mine" in this case doesn't refer to an explosive that blows up when stepped upon, but rather to the process of tunneling underneath fortress walls and then detonating explosives directly beneath them. The Turkish army had attempted this during the siege of Constantinople, but at that time they hadn't owned a unit competent enough to tunnel its way accurately to a destination. As their empire expanded to encompass the Balkans, however, they began using mining engineers from the numerous silver mines in the region, and Turkish military engineering took a great leap forward. At any rate, the tunnel had to pass under a moat that was twenty meters deep. It needed to be begun from quite a distance away—partly to avoid detection by the defenders who would notice the large crowd of laborers that the effort involved.

On September 3rd, beneath the outer wall that girded the English Fort, the Turks exploded their first mine. At the same time, they stepped up their artillery barrage. For the first time since the siege began, the invaders were able to spill into the moat and advance their attack. Mustafa Pasha could be seen issuing orders on the rim of the moat as he commanded the attack. One-third of the outer wall had been blown apart, revealing naked earth and exposing a tunnel that was a full two meters wide. The defenders retreated to the inner fortress wall, hoping to draw the Turks who had forced their way in over the rubble as close as possible in order to fell them with small arms and crossbows at point blank range. The assault was on the Englishmen's wall, but French and Castilian knights soon rushed to their aid.

That day, Mustafa Pasha committed all 20,000 troops under his command to the assault. Although the defenders numbered less than one-tenth of that, the knights were elite soldiers who had been living in a state of constant readiness. Battle-hardened warriors are formidable. The Turkish army's first major assault ended in retreat as the sun set. The Turks suffered about two thousand deaths, while the defenders' losses numbered only three knights and a smattering of troops; they had been sent flying when the mine detonated right under the outer wall they had been defending.

The defenders became keenly aware of the immediate need to take fundamental countermeasures against mines. After all, the enemy had been able to dig a two-meter-wide tunnel without their knowledge. A plan that the engineer Martinengo had devised beforehand was implemented immediately. The women, children, and elderly of the city were mobilized and provided with a tool of his design. It was a brilliantly simple device: a half-drum with a thin layer of sheepskin equipped with small hanging balls of cork. When these drums were placed against the wall of the trench dug along the inside of the fortifications, they detected even the faintest sounds originating underground and amplified them as the cork bounced against the sheepskin. These were, in short, rudimentary ultrasonic sensors, and the townsfolk happily took part in the plan. It soon became evident that children's ears were particularly keen.

Using this method they detected twelve mines in September alone. Digging their own tunnels to meet their enemies', they successfully removed the explosives in them before they could be detonated. The Turkish army conducted their tunneling operations during the daytime, while their artillery was thundering away, but the defenders could also tunnel during the night. Martinengo's idea to attach roofs to the trenches not only saved the children from the dust raised by the cannons but had the added advantage, greater than expected, of dampening the noise of the blasts as the civilians strove to detect the enemy's tunneling activity.

Not all of the Turkish mines failed to explode, however. As for the cannons, they hurled one hundred shots a day by the middle of September. An average of twelve mortar rounds rained daily on each of the ramparts defended by the knights of Italy, Provence, England, and Aragon. Although the Turks suffered far more casualties than the defenders, their numbers gradually kept increasing. The destruction dealt to the outer walls defended by Aragon and England was particularly appalling, so much so that men could no longer be stationed on them.

Nonetheless, the defenders still had five forts from which they could deploy a new weapon that served well to repel enemy soldiers attacking the ramparts. A variation on "Greek fire," it was a primitive flamethrower that shot flames out of a long tube. Its shortcoming was that it couldn't be used for an extended period, but this was remedied by having spares at the ready. Turkish soldiers were lightly equipped and most didn't even wear steel breastplates. Once they were enveloped in flames, it was over for them.

Although the defenders continued to fight bravely, they had for some time been unable to obtain accurate information about the enemy—the hardest part of having to fight while totally cut off from the outside world. The leadership of the order had enjoyed an excellent grasp of the Turks' situation prior to their initial landfall but had received absolutely no new intelligence in the month and a half since the completion of their encampment at the end of July. All present at the war council recognized this need and debated measures to address it.

One remarked that sending a Greek Rhodian to infiltrate the enemy's ranks was out of the question, and everyone concurred. As a Greek and member of the subjugated class of Rhodes, such a man couldn't be expected to choose death over disclosure if he were captured. Moreover, there was always the chance he could be turned into a double agent for the Turks. There were a large number of ethnic Greeks serving in the Turkish army, all of them Ottoman subjects. A Greek would have made an ideal spy in terms of language and ethnicity, but the knights had to abandon the idea. Yet a Western European would risk detection because of his physical appearance.

Infiltration

The council eventually decided to send two Italian-born knights. One was a nobleman from the prosperous southern Italian region of Puglia, which had once been a colony of ancient Greece. His nose angled straight down from his forehead, a type not uncommon in Greece even today. He also had swarthy skin, black eyes, and black hair. Very few would doubt that he was Greek. It also certainly helped that he was fluent in Greek.

The other man was Orsini. Nobody had any doubt that if Orsini were captured he would die before saying a word. His daring and belligerent attitude towards the Turkish enemy was also common knowledge. The Grand Master made the bold claim that Orsini would refuse to return until he had seen everything there was to see, not overlooking anything of importance. But there were many disadvantages in choosing the young knight from Rome. To begin with, he had flaxen hair and ashen eyes bearing a touch of blue. His translucent skin was somewhat ruddy even when tanned by the sun, a characteristic of young Western Europeans.

Orsini smiled radiantly when informed of the decision and immediately returned to his home. He made another appearance in the chambers of the council about an hour later. Those who saw him were astounded. This knight from the highest ranks of the Roman aristocracy had completely transformed himself into a Greek commoner. His soft, wavy, flaxen hair had transformed into ringlets of burnt umber. His ruddy but lightly tanned skin had been blackened. His gray-blue eyes hadn't changed, except now they just added to the impression that he was a Greek from the Black Sea region rather than a Turk. His clothing, wherever he had found it, gave him a coarse appearance. It was completely appropriate attire for a deckhand on a Greek ship. Orsini's disguise impressed everyone, and they all wholeheartedly entrusted him with the important task. He had to keep completely quiet amidst the enemy, however, since he wasn't fluent in Greek. All the talking would be done by the knight from Puglia.

A small boat carrying the two disguised men secretly

exited the harbor in the middle of the night. Six Greek sailors who had long worked for the order were rowing. These men also had an important and difficult job. After leaving the two knights on the eastern coast of the island, they were to continue southward to the base at Lindos, where they were to wait two days; on the night of the third day, they would return to the spot where they had dropped off the knights in order to sneak them back into the port of Rhodes. Like the knights, they were dressed as lower-class Greeks. The small boat, however, flew a Turkish flag.

The Turks appeared to intensify their barrage with each passing day. They had not only increased their number of cannons but also truncated the time between each cannon's discharge. The outer wall of the Spanish Fort had been transformed into a pile of sand and stone, and only a third of the outer wall of the English Fort remained standing. Nevertheless, the main fortress walls were still perfectly intact, and not one enemy soldier had been able to crawl over them. These walls had so far escaped any damage from mines, but no one doubted that tunnels were being dug toward many of them. A mine had destroyed half the outer wall of the Italian section, which had long gone spared.

The leadership of the order had assembled in a hall of the Grand Master's Palace, the highest point in the city. The two knights sent into the enemy camp were supposed to return that very night and report directly to that chamber as soon as their boat entered harbor. The wait, however, was a long one. Even after the candles had burned down and were replaced by new ones, the pair still had not returned. Antonio, pacing back and forth atop the Italian wall on watch, was one of those who awaited Orsini that night. The lamps of every room at the residence of the Italian division, which had sent off two of its own on a very perilous mission, remained lit long after midnight.

The Debriefing

The second set of candles had burned down to small stumps and were about to flicker out when the two knights finally appeared. Both men were so filthy that they had no need for disguises, and so exhausted they seemed on the verge of collapse. Orsini began by explaining they'd had trouble sneaking out of the laborers' quarters where they had been billeted. Since they had not brought weapons and would be conspicuous amongst the soldiers, they had procured tools and mingled in with the laborers. Working, they had observed the enemy.

Orsini, who held the higher rank within the order, delivered most of the report. The knight from Puglia only opened his mouth when Orsini requested confirmation and to answer questions from the council. Orsini's manner of speaking remained unchanged even though he was completely exhausted. He spoke of his feat nonchalantly as though it had been performed by another, and occasionally expressed himself with smiles and even mild laughter.

The knights had infiltrated the enemy camp unnoticed and joined a company of laborers that was brusquely beaten awake at dawn. The workers came from a wide variety of locales and it was simply understood that they couldn't communicate with one another. The fact that Orsini could not speak Greek, or that his companion could speak Greek but not Turkish, was not a cause for worry. The vast size of the Ottoman Empire made this perfectly normal.

The two knights spent the first day constructing a makeshift dock on a sandy beach. This wasn't a new project, but rather an attempt to reinforce a pre-existing structure whose foundation had collapsed because of unsound assembly. The labor conscripts were forced to begin work at the crack of dawn, and only at sunset did they return to their crude tents for a night's rest. Their rations consisted of nothing more than black bread, water, and one plate of steamed vegetables. Meat and fruit were not theirs. Most of the men used in construction had been conscripted from near the Danube River. Turkish soldiers supervised their work during the day and allowed them no freedom at night. Squads of Turks made nightly patrols of the tents pitched along the seashore. It seemed they had to take steps to keep even putative subjects of their state from escaping.

On the second day of their infiltration, right before the summons at dawn, the knights succeeded in making their way into Mustafa Pasha's camp facing the English Fort. There, too, they joined a group of laborers and began digging a mine.

The entrance to the tunnel was dug out nearly a hundred meters from the precipice of the moat. The workers started digging at a slight diagonal and then continued in a direct horizontal line towards the fortress wall. Orsini reported it had been too dangerous to try to count how many different tunnels were being dug in the entire area; Turkish soldiers with drawn swords were always present, supervising the work. Both knights could testify with certainty, however, that there were ten tunnels for the English wall alone. One of these seemed headed for the English Fort itself, which had put even Orsini into a cold sweat. The enemy, faced with an impregnable stronghold, planned to blow it up foundation and all.

The moment he heard this, the Grand Master turned to Martinengo, a signal to the two knights to pause for a moment. Martinengo immediately laid a piece of paper on the table and began drawing lines with his ruler. His plan was to dig two tunnels at the same time, one coming from the Aragonese wall and the other from the English. He calculated that these two would intersect with the Turkish tunnel directly in front of the English Fort. Nobody made a sound as Martinengo completed the diagram.

He handed it over to La Vallette, the Grand Master's secretary. No further instructions were required. One of La Vallette's servants immediately ran it to the residence of the Italian knights, where he entrusted it to Martinengo's two assistants. Engineers who took part in siege defense always had people and machinery prepared for just such a contingency, and the plan was immediately put into operation. Grand Master L'Isle-Adam knew this to be the case and felt a measure of relief once the diagram had left the chamber. He urged Orsini to continue his report. Orsini resumed speaking, occasionally asking his partner to corroborate this or that point.

An Unforeseen Development

As their work was ending around sunset of the second day, the two knights faced the prospect of spending a night in the work unit's huts at the outskirts of the camp. Knowing that the huts were locked from the outside at night, they decided to make their escape before the workday came to an end.

Pushing a cart loaded with soil, they crossed the enemy encampment facing the Aragonese wall, passing by the sultan's tent, and reached the area outside the Auvergne wall, where the Janissaries were based. They abandoned the cart and joined a group that was busily constructing an artillery platform.

The tents of the laborers in that area were ordered to be illuminated at night. They were not far from where the Turkish army had been concentrating its attacks, and even the laborers' tents were pitched near the front line. The knights saw this as a good opportunity to inspect the front line and snuck their way into one of the tents closest to the front. With their heads sticking out of the tent as if the heat was unbearable and they needed to cool off, the knights stayed awake and observed their surroundings.

It was around midnight when Orsini noticed something flash directly ahead of him in the dark above the Fort of St. Georges. He got his companion's attention, and two sets of eyes were watching as a second flash appeared. This happened five more times at fixed intervals. Neither of the knights had any doubt—someone was sending signals to the Turkish camp from atop the fort. They waited a while longer, but there were no more flashes. The tent of Agra Pasha, commander of the Janissaries, was between them and the moat, though closer to the moat. The knights saw a Turkish soldier dash out of that tent towards that of the sultan.

There was a spy amongst them. There was an enemy spy within the fortress walls of Rhodes. Upon learning this, everyone in the council froze.

Orsini continued to explain that they spent all of the following day trying to extract themselves from the perilous depths of the Ottoman camp. He told of how they reached the distant rendezvous point on the coast, where they were picked up by the boat, and how they returned to the port of Rhodes. No one was listening. Everybody was preoccupied with thoughts of the spy in their midst. When the two knights completed their report, all the Grand Master could manage was an absentminded "well done."

They had to take immediate steps against this espionage. Without discussing it first with the council, the Grand Master appointed a knight to investigate the matter. This was quite unusual for L'Isle-Adam, who made a practice of asking for his colleagues' opinions even when his mind was already made up. L'Isle-Adam himself seemed unaware that he was acting out of character.

The investigation was entrusted to an English knight, Sir William Norfolk. He was commander of the order's navy and so was present at the council. Nobody objected to his appointment.

Norfolk was a veteran knight who had lived on Rhodes for many years. He spoke Greek, of course, but his Turkish was also passable. He had learned the language while working as an oarsman on a galley ship after having been taken prisoner and sold into slavery. His long years of experience as a ship's captain had also made him quite adept at dealing with the common people of Rhodes, who were seafarers. Indeed, they held him in high esteem. Since it was unthinkable for a member of the order to be sending secret messages to the enemy, L'Isle-Adam wanted the investigation to start with the Greek populace.

The Grand Master instructed all present that they were not to utter a single word about anything they had discussed that night. It was imperative to exercise the utmost discretion during the investigation.

The assembled knights dispersed to return to their posts, not allowing themselves a moment's sleep. The first rays of dawn were already flooding the room through the window facing the sea.

A Volcano Floating in the Sea

The siege was entering its third month as the southern isle entered autumn. The first three days following the meeting brought an unprecedented concentration of cannonballs and mines. The barrage struck ramparts guarded by Italy, England, Provence, and Aragon, the entire southern stretch of the fortress. Mines now exploded frequently in the dark. The defenders could no longer operate with reduced numbers on nighttime guard.

Worse, they were having difficulty with their mine countermeasures. No matter how good they got at detecting the tunnels, the enemy countered by digging even more of them. Thus outnumbered, the defenders simply couldn't keep pace. Furthermore, the inner trench that had served to detect and thus foil the mines was now subjected to showers of rocks and earth that crashed through its roof, debris from the walls themselves, which by this time were noticeably damaged. The area was no longer safe for children with tunnel-detection drums. Martinengo's devices were no longer much use, anyway, since the explosions of mines, even at night, made it impossible to detect the fainter sounds of tunneling.

The horrible intensity of the three-day assault not

only terrified the populace inside the fortress walls, but also shocked those outside of Rhodes. The knights defending Kos and Bodrum dispatched ships to gather reports on the situation. The scouts watching from sea compared Rhodes, shrouded in smoke and ringing with the constant roar of explosions, to a volcano suddenly risen out of the water. During those three days, the defenders were bombarded with fifteen hundred cannon rounds and suffered twelve successful mine detonations.

Everyone expected the Turks to follow up with an all-out attack.

The Turkish army, as a rule, executed the same strategy in every single battle. They would start with a massive artillery barrage to demolish the defenders' fortifications. At the same time they would start tunneling to lay mines. When the mines began producing results, they would step up the pace of the artillery. Once the defense had been sufficiently softened, they launched an all-out attack using their entire force. In that era, when even Charles, the most powerful monarch in Western Europe, could only muster twenty thousand men, the ability to execute such a strategy was unique to the Ottoman Sultan, who could summon a hundred thousand.

It was also customary for the three days before the full assault to be used to rest for it. Excepting the artillerymen and the engineers, every soldier was exempted from all duty other than sharpening his weapon. He was instructed to rest his mind and body as much as possible; at the same time, he was expected to observe an almost complete fast. If his spirit did not rise inexorably in preparation for the full attack, he was no Islamic warrior. War against heretics was supposed to be a sublime and exalted opportunity to receive the blessings of Allah.

At any given time, however, a third of the soldiers in the Turkish army were non-Muslim. Most of these were Greek Orthodox Christians living under Turkish rule. While the Turks were tolerant in matters of religion and didn't expect these conscripts to experience spiritual exaltation prior to offering their lives to Allah, the three days of near fasting held for them, too.

The Orthodox Christians knew the Turkish strategy full well, and knew without being told what was expected of them once the assault commenced. They would carry out the first wave of the attack. This, too, was customary in the Ottoman army.

Full Frontal Assault

The sounds of flutes, drums, and bugles filled the air in the Turkish camp before the sun rose on September 24th. The music began in front of the English Fort, and quickly spread in a curve around the ramparts of Provence, Italy, and Aragon. Since the music signaled the origin of an offensive, the defenders would be attacked from virtually all of the landward sides of the fortress.

During the previous two months, the Turks had launched a total of five attacks. They had been directed at the ramparts of Italy, Provence, England, and Aragorn, but only one wall at a time. Today would mark the first simultaneous attack from all sides.

Alarm bells began sounding throughout the city, calling the defenders to their posts. Once the church bells started their raucous clanging, not only the knights and mercenaries, but also the reservists drawn from the city's commoners rushed to their battle stations. The Castilian and French knights assigned to the seaward walls rushed to the aid of their comrades facing land. Their vacated posts would be filled by the crew of Western European merchant vessels that had been trapped in the harbor.

A somewhat smaller golden tent appeared that day, easily visible from the fortress walls. It was on an elevated stand in front of Koskinou Fort, precisely in the center of the front. The sultan would use it to oversee the battlefield. Four viziers were each at his post by the edge of the moat from where, mounted on a splendid Arab stallion, he would command his troops. On the defenders' side, the Grand Master himself appeared atop the walls next to a great battle flag bearing the white cross against a field of red.

The enemy's all-out attack opened with a foray by the Christian irregulars. They had been fully occupied with tunneling and other construction tasks for the past two months and were only outfitted with a jumble of mismatching uniforms and weapons. They had no choice but to march forward, looking as if they were being thrust out of the moat and into the battle. The Janissaries were behind them at the bottom of the moat, swords drawn, waiting to cut down any who should try to turn back.

The artillery barrage was halted. All that could be heard were the raised voices of the invading troops, yet it was unclear whether these were battle cries or screams of terror. In no time at all the attackers had filled the moat and were now pouring through the gaps in the crumbling outer wall. Yet they continued advancing only because they were more afraid of going back than going forward. Those who made it to the walls leaned their ladders against them and attempted to climb. Those without ladders latched onto the walls and started scaling up like lizards.

The defenders countered with cool and unerring precision. Since they couldn't afford to waste munitions or manpower, they had to allow the enemy soldiers to come as close as possible before dispatching them. The troops defending the forts were nearly prostrate as they toppled the thronging enemy soldiers.

When the sunlight had finally warmed the day, the irregulars were given the order to withdraw. Nearly three thousand corpses were left behind at the sound of the retreat bugle. Then, with no rest and without even attending to the dead or wounded, the second wave of the assault commenced. This time it was the regular Turkish army, who at least had matching weapons and uniforms. They attacked the walls using more than simple ladders, but the second they affixed anything to the walls or forts it was burned off by the defenders' flamethrowers. Against these regular troops the knights also used a kind of hand grenade made of small terra-cotta jars filled with gunpowder. Turkish solders were not in the habit of wearing steel armor and were thus virtually defenseless against fire. Even his comrades had to back away from any soldier whose body had turned into a ball of fire.

Nevertheless, this was the sultan's regular army, and it did not launch reckless attacks. Their method of assault was uniform and disciplined. Moreover, the sheer number of them, at 50,000 men, overwhelmed the defenders.

News that the enemy flag had been raised over the Spanish Fort sped across the ramparts. The Grand Master hurriedly led the reserve of knights to that fort; at the same time, he received news that the situation atop the Italian wall had degenerated into a melee with enemy troops who had managed to scale the slopes. Knights rushing to and fro filled the ten-meter-wide passageway atop the walls. The Turks had probably noticed the deterioration in the defense of the area between the English and Spanish Forts. It was there that they committed the elite Janissaries, who numbered 15,000. Mustafa Pasha was now in charge of 20,000 regulars augmented by 15,000 Janissaries.

Intense battle continued to rage all across the front, but the fiercest fighting took place at the wall being attacked by the Janissaries. Even the order's battle flag, which served to show the location of the Grand Master, couldn't be raised there. The Janissaries' ferocity that day confirmed their reputation for bravery, a bravery that made them the backbone of the Turkish army.

The corps of Janissaries was composed of men who were forcibly recruited, as boys of seven or eight, from Christian lands under Turkish rule. After being converted to Islam, they lived communally and trained together as warriors. They were not allowed to have wives, nor could they own homes. They obeyed only Allah and his earthly agent, the sultan. The strength of the elite Janissaries lay in their unique psychology; with no parents or families of their own, they were bound only to the sultan. This made them even more fanatical than native Turks. Since they were not Muslims by birth, they felt a conscious need to prove repeatedly and forcefully that they were indeed true Muslims. This fanaticism proved most effective to the Turks when battling a Christian foe.

The fighting finally ended that day after more than six hours. Ultimately, the knights had managed to hold the walls, but the moat was packed with corpses after the enemy withdrew. While the Turkish casualties were said to have numbered ten thousand, the defenders counted three hundred and fifty dead and five hundred wounded. Antonio del Carretto was among the latter.

The Turks began the task of carrying off the dead and wounded while the sun still shone on the moat. The defenders didn't shoot a single arrow at them. Whether they were on the walls or in the forts, the knights and other combatants, after such a fierce battle, lay unmoving as if dead. No one celebrated with cheers of victory.

In his tent, Sultan Suleiman exploded in rage at the six commanders kneeling before him with heads hung low. He laid blame for the failed assault on Mustafa Pasha. Suleiman imagined himself a man of law and a monarch who defended order. He was always self-conscious about being only twenty-eight-years old, and therefore up to that time had proceeded with extreme caution. Still, he had firmly believed that the single full-scale attack would put victory firmly in his grasp. But even after two full months of slow and deliberate preparation, the climactic strike, with a force twenty times that of the defenders, had ended in miserable failure. At this moment Suleiman, who had always taken great pains to be calm in his dealings with others, seemed to remember exactly who held absolute power in the Ottoman Empire. Mustafa Pasha may have been his Grand Vizier and brother-in-law, but that did not exempt him from taking responsibility for the defeat.

Suleiman sentenced Mustafa Pasha to death. When Kazim Pasha pleaded for clemency on Mustafa's behalf, saying that the sentence was too harsh, he was sentenced to death as well.

Though quivering with fear, all the other commanders voiced their objections. They stated that the battlefront would fall apart if Kazim, the oldest and most experienced of the viziers, and Mustafa, the Grand Vizier, were put to death. This reasoning, in the end, brought Suleiman around. He would allow Kazim to retain his position in the battle line, but Mustafa was demoted to Governor of Syria. He would leave Rhodes early the following morning, leading twenty ships to his new post. A man from Greece named Ibrahim—just one year older than Suleiman and a close aide—replaced Mustafa Pasha on the front. The Grand Vizier's post was left vacant for the time being, but one year later this very Ibrahim would be vying for the position.

The Wound

Antonio del Carretto had collapsed atop the Italian wall. He had been firing his crossbow at enemy soldiers scrambling up the wall when a bullet came out of nowhere and slammed into his shoulder, sending him reeling. His steel armor wasn't pierced by the bullet, but it didn't lessen the force of the impact. The enemy took advantage of that moment of vulnerability. A Turkish soldier who had scurried over the wall leapt upon him while he was still staggering from the hit. The unsheathed dagger in the Turk's left hand pierced Antonio's right groin as he fell backwards. Burning pain burst through the lower half of his body, but he had no time to attend to it; the Turkish soldier's face hovered directly over the narrow opening of his steel helmet. When he saw sunlight glimmer off the tip of the scimitar poised in the Turk's right hand, he thought it was the end. Although steel armor was effective when the wearer had freedom of movement, as soon as that was lost, its weight and intricacy worked against him. It was practical when fighting at a distance, but not when the enemy had just tackled you.

Antonio expected the Turk to cut his head off at that instant, but instead the Turk froze and then slumped over. Before Antonio knew it, somebody was dragging him down the passageway of the rampart and still further down the inner stone staircase. It was not until Antonio was well clear of the wall that he recognized the voice of the person ordering one of the soldiers to take Antonio to the hospital. It was Orsini.

There were so many wounded in the hospital that they had spilled out into the inner courtyard. Even so, Antonio was given a spot in the cloisters, no doubt because he wore the armor of a knight. There, at least, he was protected from the sunlight, which was fierce despite the season. One of the doctors making rounds came to his side. By that time, Antonio's heavy armor had already been removed, and the blood flowing from his open wound had left dark stains in his leggings. The doctor ordered a nurse to cut the leggings open and then started to dress the wound. Antonio didn't recall anything that happened after that, surely a result of excessive blood loss. When he regained consciousness, he found himself lying on a bed in a private room in the hospital, his personal valet standing next to him with a look of concern. His lower body was practically paralyzed with severe pain. He was so delirious with fever that he could barely form a coherent thought.

He thought of his mother, Peretta. She was still young, having only been eighteen when she gave birth to him. Her features were not markedly beautiful, but she struck people as beautiful nonetheless. She was a cultured woman and had seen to Antonio's early education. More importantly, she seemed like the personification of life itself. She lit up a room just by walking into it. The Marquise del Carretto was the flower of Genoese society, and even her maids were proud of their mistress.

She had three sons. Giovanni was the eldest and one year older than Antonio; Marco was born two years after Antonio. While she was not one to play favorites, she had kept Antonio, the most handsome and gentle of the three, constantly by her side. Antonio was sometimes confused by his mother's sweet and mild fragrance as he was growing up, yet, if he did not sense it for a while, he would feel that something was lacking. Antonio never felt nostalgic for his father or brothers, but at times he couldn't but long intensely for his mother, Peretta. It was an emptiness that was not so much emotional, however, as physical.

It was nearly evening when Orsini came to look in on him. Antonio opened his eyes upon hearing the clanking of armor and recognized his friend in the doorway. Orsini was holding his helmet in the steel glove of his left hand. He passed the valet, who had withdrawn to the alcove respectfully, and approached the bed. Orsini bent down on one knee to get as close to Antonio as possible. The soft clanging of armor filled the air for an instant.

"The doctor said the wound is not serious." Orsini was smiling as he peered at Antonio. He had come without bothering to wash first, so his face and armor were still soiled with mud and blood. The sweet and pungent smell of Orsini's sweat enveloped Antonio, who said nothing as he looked to his friend for support.

The smile faded from the Roman knight's lips, but a trace of it remained in his gray-blue eyes. He stretched out his open right hand and lightly touched Antonio's forehead. He smoothed Antonio's hair, then paused for a moment before standing, once again causing his armor to clang.

"I'll come back tomorrow," he said, and then left the room. As the sound of the armor grew fainter, Antonio felt himself descend into a peaceful slumber the likes of which he had never before experienced.

Martinengo Falls

The Turkish attacks again intensified with the arrival of October. An all-out attack was no longer a rarity, coming at ten-day intervals. There was no time for the defenders to rest during that interval. Passing with the speed of arrows, the days were consumed with efforts to cope with the artillery barrages and the mines. In truth, they no longer had any effective countermeasures. They could only repair the collapsed sections in solemn silence. Had they stopped to consider the actual effectiveness of this, they probably would have given up in despair.

Nevertheless, the inhabitants continued to cooperate in the defense. They still remembered the fear they had experienced when the Turkish army first arrived. Their motivations may have been different, but the knights and the civilians had an interest in common. This permitted the combatants, including the mercenaries, to focus solely on the fighting. The women of Rhodes gathered and transported the materials necessary to repair the walls and the forts, while the men carried out the repairs. The people did their work with astonishing composure given the difficulty of their situation. Martinengo was directly in charge of the repairs, which made his wounding an especially serious blow to the defenders. The Grand Master even grew pale when he heard the news.

In the afternoon of October 11th, an enemy arrow pierced Martinengo's right eye. He hadn't been wearing his heavy helmet as he found it inconvenient for making inspections and giving orders.

Antonio, who could now walk with the aid of a cane, was in the corridor overlooking the courtyard in front of his room when a group carrying a wounded man rushed in the first floor entrance. There were so many people around the man that Antonio couldn't see him from where he was on the second floor. Since the man had been brought in with great urgency and all of the doctors attending to other patients around the courtyard rushed at once to treat him, Antonio assumed he was a very high-ranking knight. Without wasting a second they carried him up the stairs to a private room on the second floor. Antonio noticed the man had no armor on his arms or legs and thought it strange that a leading knight would only be wearing a breastplate. It then occurred to him that this might be the Venetian engineer with whom he had arrived on the island. In no time at all, Grand Master L'Isle-Adam himself, his face looking even sterner than usual, went into the private room with a number of knights in tow. By that time the entire hospital knew about Martinengo's injury. He no longer had a right eyeball, only a mass of blood in its place. The doctors said it would be impossible to restore vision to that eye, but at least his life was not in danger.

The engineer, a mere commoner of the Venetian Republic, showed so much strength of will that he astonished even the noblest of the Western European blue-bloods. It was Martinengo, not the Grand Master, who reassured the knights that this was not an insuperable setback; by the very next day, he had turned his hospital room into an office.

As he lay in bed, his face half covered with bandages, one of his two assistants sat constantly by his side drawing diagrams and writing out orders as directed. The other assistant oversaw the construction on site. Whenever damage was sustained, a messenger ran to the hospital with a report. Martinengo's room became the busiest in the hospital; Antonio could only look on in awe and admiration from his room on the opposite side of the cloister.

Despite Martinengo's incredible willpower, however, his injury did have negative consequences. As the days went by, the holes in the fortifications kept getting larger. The damage to the Aragonese wall was so severe on October 20th that in some places, lacking sufficient stones and sandbags, it had to be reinforced with hastily constructed wooden fences. When the Turks immediately burnt that fence, the pitiful state of repairs became widely apparent. Martinengo could only grit his teeth as their best efforts were proven useless.

The damage to the fortifications merely accumulated, far exceeding what Martinengo could handle from his hospital room. The misery of the defenders was compounded when the net of the spy investigation spread in an unexpected direction.

The Traitor

The top-secret investigation being conducted by the English knight Norfolk finally snagged a prey on October 26th. A number of suspects had been considered, but in the end the culprit was caught red-handed trying to shoot off an arrow with a letter to the Turks.

He was a Jewish doctor working in the hospital. The Jewish people had everywhere been treated as outsiders since losing their homeland and dispersing from the Eastern Mediterranean toward Western Europe. It made sense for them to pursue professions that could provide a livelihood even if they were persecuted and driven from their homes with only the shirts on their backs. Education in Jewish families, for this reason, centered around intellectual professions such as medicine. If such practices are pursued across a span of generations, chances are that a significant pool of top talent will be cultivated. If Jews had been removed from the ranks of physicians during the Middle Ages and the Renaissance, there would have been almost nobody to take their place. This would have held true in both Christendom and Muslim lands.

Historically, the Order of the Knights of St. John had two fundamental missions, medicine and warfare. The knights themselves handled the warfare, but the medicine had to be left to others. There is no evidence showing that the nobles of Western Europe aspired to the practice of medicine. One rare exception was Venice, where being an aristocrat was predicated on greatness in commerce, not on ownership of land. In any event, it was not at all odd for all the doctors in a hospital to be Jewish, even in the hospital of a proudly Christian order of knights. Jewish doctors were paid for their expertise; nobody made an issue of their religious beliefs. Disqualifying a candidate because he was Jewish would have meant closing all the hospitals.

Yet no matter how talented a Jewish person may have been, he would not have been given military duties. He would not have been trusted for the simple reason that he had no homeland for which he was willing to die. The Knights of St. John never confided in their physicians about military affairs.

Yet, the note attached to the arrow contained information ranging from the size of the order's gunpowder stores to the number of working cannons. The doctor obviously hadn't been working alone. He revealed his co-conspirator under torture and insisted that he himself was nothing more than a messenger. He was simply following the other's orders by passing on the information to the enemy. He identified the man as Diaz.

Diaz was apprehended and immediately tortured. He was the Portuguese servant of the head of the Castilian residence, Andrea Dal Mare, who was second in rank only to the Grand Master himself. As soon as the torture began, Diaz confessed that he had taken letters to the Jewish doctor. He claimed, however, that it was only on the direct orders of his master and asserted total ignorance of the content of those letters.

The leaders of the order turned white. The wretched spy was one of their own. Not only that, he was the ranking lieutenant of the order privy to all of the council's deliberations. The very essence of a knight in the Order of St. John was his honor as a nobleman and his mission, indeed his calling, to rid the world of the infidel. That such a man would secretly send information to the Turkish enemies of Christ threw the knights into a state of despair, rage, and profound sadness.

Dal Mare was arrested on October 28th and taken to the highest room in the Fort of St. Nicholas, the fortress that jutted out into the sea. There the Portuguese knight was interrogated, but he refused to say a word. Nothing they did to him, including torture, could make him break his silence. It seemed he knew nothing he could say would do him any good, so he said nothing at all. There were neither pleas nor words of denial. When Diaz was brought in to repeat his confession in his master's presence, Dal Mare simply said, "You are a coward."

The testimony against Dal Mare mounted. There were those who said that when Dal Mare had been given command of the fleet along with the current Grand Master L'Isle-Adam when both had been mid-level knights, the two had argued numerous times over tactical matters. On top of that, Dal Mare had been a powerful rival for the position of Grand Master that eventually went to L'Isle-Adam. Someone testified that, after suffering defeat in the election, Dal Mare had said, "L'Isle-Adam will be the last Grand Master to occupy the Isle of Rhodes." There was even something in his everyday attitude and behavior that people found disagreeable. He was standoffish and not very popular among the knights.

Nevertheless, there was no material evidence against him. His continued silence, however, surely provoked the knights, who were already exhausted by the siege. On November 3rd, the council voted unanimously to sentence all of the traitors to death. The doctor and the servant were to die by hanging, while the knight would be beheaded.

On November 4th, the executions were carried out in the courtyard in front of the Grand Master's Palace. Dal Mare was the last of the three to be killed. He died without receiving the blessing due a Christian, having refused the offer of last rites. He said nothing to the very end.

Not all of the members of the order agreed with the council's decision. No one voiced any objections, but several of the knights found it impossible to dispel their doubts about Dal Mare's guilty verdict. Orsini was one of them. When he visited Antonio's hospital room, Antonio made sure they were alone before quietly asking him about it. The young Roman knight looked at Antonio, paused for a moment, and then simply replied: "I don't know."

The heads of the traitors were hung facing the enemy from the Fort of St. Georges, the site from which they had passed on crucial secrets. Their dead bodies were quartered and burned. No records remain to tell us how the Turks responded.

The seasonal rains were due even on this southern island.

Deaths Consecrated to Christ

In the Order of the Knights of St. John, it didn't matter whether a knight died in battle or of disease, or if his remains were lost—his name was not officially remembered. All that was recorded was the number of knights who were summoned by Christ on a given date. Exceptions were made for Grand Masters and other high-ranking knights; their passing was frequently documented. News was sent to their families, and sometimes monuments were even built in their honor. This, however, was not the order's official policy, but rather, nothing more than the last respects of friends and family. Moreover, such gestures were normally reserved for times of peace and not indulged during wartime unless a resolution to the conflict was seen as imminent. A number of monuments to the knights remain on Rhodes even today. Some knights were fortunate enough to be thus memorialized after having fallen in battle, but there were many who weren't.

This custom of anonymity was shared by monastic orders. It originated in the idea of dedicating one's whole life to the service of God and Christ. To die for Christ and then to leave a record of one's name was blasphemy. A soul was expected to abandon his name upon becoming God's servant and was naturally expected to remain nameless upon dying.

The silver dishes embossed with the coats of arms of Europe's illustrious families, the beautifully embroidered bed sheets—all of these were given to the hospital for use by the patients once a knight died. In time, these, too, would wear out and become unusable. With that, all traces of their former owners would disappear for all time.

Even the number of people who had died on a given date was frequently listed inaccurately in the order's records. The knights clearly didn't consider record-keeping an act of great importance. Records are kept with the thought that they will be of use in the future. The greater their perceived utility, the more detailed they tend to be. The Italian cities of Venice, Genoa, and Florence left the most detailed and accurate data of their time. While they were certainly not trying to aid the historical research of later generations, it was important for these states, whose economic foundations were commerce, finance, and industry, to acquire the latest information. They had come to understand that, as far as information was concerned, nothing was more important than meticulous and accurate record-keeping and safe storage. They were inclined even to set down things that seemed irrelevant at first glance.

An organization such as the Order of the Knights of St. John, on the other hand, was indifferent to such economic principles. The knights lived off of donated real estate, profit derived from that real estate, and income from piracy. The members of the order were scions of the aristocracy proud of their special status. They had no interest in swelling their ranks through indiscriminate recruitment. Add to that the monastic principle of abandoning one's name, and the importance of bookkeeping further decreases. The only way to trace individual members of such an organization is to seek out the private records that those individuals may have left behind.

The order consisted only of nobles, and particularly of feudal lords. Even with a pitched battle involving the entire organization, it is impossible to determine accurately how many knights died in action, or even how many knights survived. If only a Venetian, or a Florentine, had taken part—but men from mercantile states such as these weren't qualified to be knights. Martinengo was born in the Venetian Republic's territory of Bergamo and was not a trueborn Venetian. Antonio del Carretto was from nobility near Genoa, not from the merchant class. Yet, while not as reliable as the detailed account that had been kept by a Venetian doctor concerning the defense of Constantinople, these two men did leave records in the form of personal correspondence.

Leaving a record, even if unintentional, is an act undertaken with an eye toward the future. Consciousness of the future signifies a certain healthiness of spirit. The Order of the Knights of St. John was perhaps one of those institutions that had dispensed with the quality from its very inception.

With every passing day in November, the Turkish attacks rapidly grew more ferocious. In Rome, even though the new pope, Adrian VI, had been coronated, he was still unable to convene the full College of Cardinals. Plague had broken out in the city and the cardinals had fled to their estates in the countryside. The pope persevered in Rome, but no one was willing to side with a non-Italian pope with no important backing. The monarchs of Western Europe, fighting amongst themselves and concerned only with their own success, would have rather seen the papal throne vacant.

Around that time, Venetian aid from Crete secretly arrived in Rhodes. Even after declaring themselves neutral, the Venetians had still arranged for a merchant ship to transport provisions. While this greatly encouraged the defenders, the same ship also brought bad news.

In response to the call for aid from the headquarters of the order, the English branch had outfitted and dispatched ships loaded with munitions. These ships had run afoul of a storm while sailing around the Iberian peninsula. The ships, the supplies, and the English knights sent as reinforcements had all been lost at sea. The Venetian ship brought no other news of relief ships, either en route or recently dispatched.

On November 22nd, at long last, the engineer Martinengo was released from the hospital and returned to the front lines after a six-week absence. The destruction to the fortifications of Rhodes, however, was now far too advanced for his return to make any difference. Antonio's wounds had also healed and he had already returned to the front in the beginning of November. What he'd seen upon his return was that the enemy had advanced their formation into the rubble of the outer walls. They were now firing their artillery from those positions.

Chapter Six

Winter 1522

Popular Unrest

Both in the Mediterranean and in Europe, winter was not considered a season suitable for battle. Although snow usually didn't fall around the Mediterranean, rain did. Spring, summer, and autumn, on the other hand, were dry, but they also brought the danger of raging plague epidemics. On more than one occasion the plague had brought a major siege to an abrupt halt. Even so, fighting in the rain presented an even greater ordeal. Campaigns were almost never continued once winter had begun.

The defending knights had their hopes riding on just that. In the winter the rains would come. The winds would blow from the south or southwest, and the seas would grow choppy. With supplies getting harder to shuttle from Asia Minor to Rhodes, the cannonade would become impossible to maintain at the same levels as in the summer. The Turkish army would suffer supply shortages. It numbered over 100,000 men, and addressing those shortages would be no easy matter. In the end, they would be forced to withdraw to Asia Minor until spring, leaving only their navy to enforce a blockade. During that hiatus the defenders could repair their fortifications and even hope for outside reinforcements.

The twenty-eight-year-old Suleiman, however, was resolved to clinch the matter. He seemed to be well aware of the defenders' circumstances. Besides, the weather on Rhodes was in fact quite mild. With enough patience, even the mud produced by the heaviest of rains would eventually dry. Furthermore, the defenders would suffer equally from the rain. If the Turkish army had to struggle to stabilize their artillery platforms, the defenders would face difficulties in repairing their walls. In light of the damage the Turks had inflicted during the four months from August to November, both in terms of human lives and fortifications, the sultan's commanders unanimously supported his decision to end it once and for all. The Turkish army was thus committed to continuing the campaign.

The unabated daily attacks made clear to the Knights that the Turks were there to stay. Near the end of November, ships bearing knights and mercenaries from the outposts of the order entered the harbor. These were the men who had been defending Kos, Bodrum, and Lindos. The Grand Master had at last been forced to order them home. He could no longer hide his sense of impending crisis. Although ships requesting aid from Western Europe were being dispatched at a rate of two per month, thus far only two ships from Naples had been promised in response.

Even during the occasional periods of heavy rain, the Turks' mine attacks continued unhindered. Repairing the walls was even more difficult after a downpour. The inhabitants of Rhodes could no longer do it all on their own; both knights and mercenaries were forced to lend a hand, leaving them no time to rest between battles.

Turks taken as prisoners of war testified that the death toll on their side had surpassed 50,000. The defenders had actually succeeded in thinning the Turkish force through a light but endless trickle of blood. The siege had lasted five months counting from July when the city had entered full defensive mode. It was four months since the first volleys. A siege of this length, in particular of a fortified city with the inhabitants present, was so rare that none could recall a precedent. Enough food had been stockpiled to last them a year, so starvation was not yet an issue. The shortage of munitions, however, was. Just as importantly, psychological fatigue was taking its toll, particularly as it became apparent that the Turks had resolved to fight throughout the winter. The people's willpower had been stretched to the limit and was ready to snap.

On the evening of November 29th, after the latest in a series of all-out attacks—without first giving it some thought, no one could say how many there'd been—a single arrow carrying a letter from the enemy camp was shot into the city. It was a letter from Suleiman addressed to the common inhabitants of Rhodes urging their surrender. If they held firm in their resistance, they would all have to prepare to be killed once the city fell.

On December 4th, a Genoese man carrying a white flag came out of the Turkish camp and climbed down into the moat in front of the Auvergne wall, yelling out a request to speak with the Grand Master. Looking up at L'Isle-Adam, who had appeared on the wall, he said that the sultan was urging them to accept an honorable surrender so the commoners' lives may be spared. The Grand

Master's one-word reply was: "Leave!"

On December 6th the Genoese man made another appearance, this time requesting permission to deliver a letter to another Genoese named Matteo who was among the besieged. Soldiers on the ramparts granted his request, but the letter he sent by arrow was not intended for Matteo. It was a letter from the sultan to the Grand Master, and its contents were no different from the verbal message two days before. L'Isle-Adam sent no reply.

On December 8th, an Albanian mercenary deserted the Fort of St. Georges, which was the closest to the enemy, and ran into the Turkish camp. He later came to the far side of the moat, shouting that he had a letter for L'Isle-Adam from Suleiman. This time the defenders didn't even pass on the missive. Afterwards, it was forbidden for anyone on the walls or forts to speak to anyone in the enemy camp.

The commoners, however, were shaken. The sultan's overtures hadn't been accompanied by any ceasefire. The artillery and mine attacks, carried out with a sort of doggedness, were by now everyday occurrences. Atop the walls, hand-to-hand combat continued unabated.

The civilian population of Rhodes could be divided into three groups: the Western European Catholic minority, the Greek Orthodox majority, and a small contingent of Jews, who could be found scattered throughout the Mediterranean. Most of the Catholic minority were Genoese, while the rest were merchants from France,

Spain, and Venice. Although technically Western European, most of them belonged to families that had lived on the island for over a hundred years and used it as a base for their trading activities with the Orient. They felt a stronger bond with Rhodes than with their motherlands. Like the Greeks and Jews, however, they didn't share the knights' willingness to die for it.

The people of Rhodes all willingly cooperated in the defense. After all, the knights were protecting them from the Muslims. Now that any such protection was in doubt, the rationale for cooperation was disappearing. In that age, the ability to provide protection was the foundation of the relationship between rulers and ruled.

Furthermore, the Greeks and Jews on Rhodes seemed to have suddenly remembered that the lands controlled by the vast Ottoman Empire supported a large number of their brethren. Sultan Suleiman's reputation as a monarch who always kept his word and abhorred senseless violence made them further inclined to contemplate surrender. The influential townsfolk of Rhodes conveyed this widespread change of heart to the local Greek Orthodox bishop.

On the evening of December 9th, while a storm raged outside, the council met in the Grand Master's Palace. Present that evening, in addition to the usual participants, were the Catholic archbishop, the Greek Orthodox bishop, and two representatives of the commoners. One of these was a Greek, the largest landholder on the island. The other was a man named Milezi from the Venetian territory of Bergamo. He had settled in Rhodes while very young, and for the past ten years had held a firm grip on the order's finances. He had traveled around the order's various real estate holdings in every part of Western Europe, collecting their revenue. He was responsible for all of the Knights' financial affairs, from selling off the spoils of piracy to paying for the construction of new galleys; he even bought all of their munitions and wheat. He knew everything about their internal affairs and could thus be counted on to snicker at any attempt at grandiloquence. Perhaps his presence was what made the debate that evening oddly subdued when one might have expected heated controversy.

The Greek Orthodox bishop explained the public's feelings. If the Knights persisted in their refusal to give up the city, the townsfolk intended to negotiate with the sultan on their own. Milezi added that the people were firm in their determination to do so and wouldn't be persuaded otherwise. He said that perhaps the sultan's offer of honorable surrender also meant that those among the besieged who wished to leave would be allowed to do so. He himself had no desire to remain in Rhodes under Turkish rule. In this, Milezi was representative of Rhodes's other long-term Western European residents.

Only one man adamantly insisted on resisting to the bitter end: La Vallette from Auvergne, the secretary to the Grand Master. His argument was that surviving by abandoning Rhodes meant relinquishing the order's *raison d'être.*

The Order of the Knights of St. John was organized in a manner very similar to the Papal State. They held open elections for the position of Grand Master under the principle of majority rule. Once elected, however, the Grand Master held absolute authority. In this sense his role was completely different from that of the Doge of the Venetian Republic, who was subject to the rule of the majority before and after he was elected. Even though the knights held discussions, in the end they had to abide by the Grand Master's decisions. A Grand Master with a strong sense of responsibility carried an especially heavy burden.

L'Isle-Adam deliberated in silence for some time. Nobody said a word. In due course, he spoke. Without directly addressing the two opposed views, he called for an objective and accurate analysis of their current defensive capabilities and the chances of outside help arriving. He would hand down his decision only after those two matters had been sufficiently examined. With that, the meeting came to a close. The storm seemed to have calmed considerably.

The Knights of St. John were faced with a choice that hadn't come before them in two hundred years. Their sole reason for existence had been to fight the infidel. If they wanted to be true to their mission, there was nothing left to do but to die fighting. They had to ignore the will of the populace and continue fighting by themselves until the last man perished. Surviving by reaching a pact with the Muslims would be a disgrace, something that had been unthinkable ever since they had made Rhodes their home. The Knights had occasionally met with the Turks under peaceful circumstances, either to contract for wheat when Rhodes was facing a shortage and Asia Minor was experiencing a surplus, or else to arrange for the exchange of prisoners. Those interactions had never left them feeling indebted to their enemies.

The Knights of St. John, who until then had held the Venetian Republic in contempt, now faced the prospect of behaving just like them. The order had been highly critical of Venice when it had signed a peace treaty with the Turks; the Venetians were scoundrels who would sell their honor as Christians for profit. When it came to piracy, the knights made no distinction between Venetian merchant ships and Turkish ships: in both cases they confiscated the merchandise and held the passengers captive, returning them only in exchange for a ransom. Muslims and those who made pacts with Muslims, even if they were Christians, were equally the enemies of Christ. Now, unless they were willing to sacrifice their very existence, the Knights themselves would fit that description. They recalled that they were the sole surviving religious order of knights. Men who lived only to wage war on Islam could think of nothing else. Saving the lives of the common inhabitants could never be of anything more than secondary importance.

Whether the sultan was aware of the unrest in the city or not, he continued writing his letters. On December 12th, two visibly high-ranking Turkish men were seen outside one of the two gates that opened inland, the one that went through Koskinou Fort and crossed over the moat. They announced they were delivering a letter from the sultan. The gate had been tightly locked throughout the siege, but the defenders opened it a crack to allow two knights to slip out and meet the messengers. The Turks handed the knights the letter and the knights went back inside. The gate was quickly shut, as tightly as before.

The Grand Master read the letter and called a meeting of the council. The two civilian representatives and the Greek Orthodox bishop were absent this time, but the seconds-in-command of each of the residences were present.

L'Isle-Adam read Suleiman's entire letter aloud to the council. It promised safe passage off the island for all members of the order and any inhabitants who wished to leave, on the condition that they relinquish the fortress. Should they continue to resist, all would be massacred when the city fell. The results of the survey of food and munitions ordered by the Grand Master were then reported. There was still several months' worth of food on hand, but less than a month's worth of munitions.

While no firm conclusion had been reached, the overall mood of the council started to lean towards giving up the city.

Peace Overtures

The Grand Master decided to make an initial offer of a three-day truce. He selected two special envoys: a knight from Auvergne said to be the most proficient in Greek of anyone in the order; and Orsini, chosen because many Turkish high officials spoke Italian thanks to their covert dealings with the mercantile city-states of Italy. Sultan Suleiman himself knew Greek well and also understood Italian. Although it was very late at night when the decision was made, the news was immediately reported to the Turkish army. Their answer accepting the envoys was relayed back that same night.

On the following day, December 13th, the two knights passed through the d'Amboise Gate, which hadn't been opened in five months, and entered the Turkish camp. At the same time, the nephew of Ahmed Pasha, along with another Turkish high official, entered the fortress through the Koskinou Gate. These two Turkish hostages were led to a room above Koskinou Gate where they were to be detained until the return of the two knights. The two envoys from the order were welcomed into the tent of one of the viziers, Ahmed Pasha, who was to serve as Suleiman's proxy in the surrender negotiations. The *pasha* showed the knights fine hospitality and the utmost courtesy even though he was in the superior position of being the party on the verge of victory. For some reason, he also seemed quite taken with Orsini. Even after the negotiations were over, he kept the knights until late into the night before allowing them to retire to their guest quarters.

The two knights learned many things during that late-night conversation. Combat fatalities in the Turkish army had climbed to 44,000 over more than four months. An almost equal number had died from disease or accidents. The Turks had detonated an astonishing total of 53 mines and had fired 85,000 rounds of artillery. Even Orsini, who was always the image of calm, couldn't but widen his eyes at hearing these numbers. The Turkish vizier credited the sultan's stubborn streak as the sole reason they could suffer such casualties and still continue to press the siege. In other words, the siege might have ended by now had the sultan not been leading it personally.

On December 14th, the two knights returned to the fortress. Two Spanish knights headed into the Turkish camp to replace them as hostages for the ceasefire.

The members of the council hastily convened to examine the peace terms that Orsini and the other knight had brought back. Suleiman promised strictly to adhere to the following conditions if the fortress were surrendered:

1. The Knights of St. John have the right to remove from the island everything they want, including all holy articles, battle flags, and sacred statues.
2. The Knights have the right to leave the island with their battle gear and possessions.

3. In the event that the order's own ships are insufficient to carry these articles, the Turkish navy will provide as many ships as necessary.
4. Everyone will be allowed twelve days to prepare for departure.
5. During that period, the Turkish army will withdraw one mile from the front line.
6. During that period, all of the order's bases outside of Rhodes must surrender.
7. All inhabitants of Rhodes who wish to leave the island will be allowed to depart freely if they do so within the following three years.
8. Those who decide to stay will be exempt from the obligatory tax levied upon all non-Turks living in Turkish-controlled territory for the next five years.
9. All Christians remaining on the island will be guaranteed complete freedom of worship.
10. Contrary to the long-standing custom of the Ottoman Empire, the children of the Christian residents of Rhodes will be exempt from recruitment into the reserves of the Janissaries.

The council had already been leaning toward surrender. The Greek residents greeted the promises in the second half of the accord with jubilation. Even the grizzled veterans among the Knights believed that the promises in the first half of the list, particularly numbers one and two that gave them the right to keep their weapons and possessions, allowed them to surrender with honor intact. The Grand Master, however, didn't seem ready to accept the agreement just yet. Another Venetian ship from Crete loaded with relief supplies was surreptitiously entering their harbor at around that time. The deliberations stretched on, and the ceasefire period lapsed before a decision could be made. The two Turkish hostages were therefore sent back out of Koskinou Gate. The Turkish army, in turn, returned the two Spanish knights.

The Turkish army nonetheless waited one more day before recommencing their artillery barrage on December 16th. The knights fought back with such ferocity that they might as well have forgotten all about the peace negotiations; however, the number of male residents who responded to the call for fighters had dramatically decreased from four days ago.

The attacks continued on December 17th. Another small ship arrived in the harbor that day from Crete. This time, though, the ship carried a letter from the Italian branch of the order. It stated that the two ships from Naples, upon which the Grand Master had placed his last hopes, were not making any advances in their preparations; it was not certain when those ships would set sail.

Death

On December 18th, a fierce attack initially focused on the half-destroyed Aragonese wall escalated into a full assault on all fronts. The Turkish attacks, however, had taken on a completely new character after the stalled peace talks. The Turks now continued their artillery fire even after their own troops were sent in to attack the walls being struck by the cannons. This didn't stop even as their own men were hit from behind and sent flying.

The Janissaries had been sent in, so the Grand Master finally ordered knights from all other walls to rush to reinforce the Aragonese section where the fighting was the worst. Ten knights were sent from the Italian wall, including Antonio and Orsini. The Grand Master himself stood on the front line, leading the reserves. The Aragonese rampart was the only place in the entire battle line where the enemy had succeeded in carving deeply into the defenders' position. If the enemy defeated them there, the whole city was in grave danger of being overrun.

Afternoon came and the battle continued to rage. The moat was filled with the corpses of Turkish soldiers, which the Janissaries stomped over as they charged toward the rubble of the battered walls. After firearms, bows, and arrows could no longer be used, a battle of swords ensued.

Evening approached. The wall suffered a direct cannon hit right where the close-quarter combat was unfolding. In fact, two rounds had struck the same spot simultaneously. The rubble and sandbags at the point of impact instantly disintegrated into a cloud of dust. Antonio was one of those flung into the air. When the dust had settled, a number of his comrades and enemy troops were lying motionless amidst the dirt and rocks. The right arm of Antonio's armor had been blown away. An eerie calm descended upon the scene in the wake of the sheer force of the impact.

Antonio shakily rose and remembered the sword he had been holding in his right hand. It had landed ten feet away. He went to pick it up. Only as he reached for it did he think of Orsini. He remembered standing nearby as his friend handily fought off two Janissaries. Terrifying images began to flood his mind as his head finally started to clear.

He could no longer think. He could only scramble around the rampart, which had been transformed into a horrible mountain of debris, searching for his friend. He found Orsini in the shade of a heap of rubble ten yards away. The left half of his body was buried under the stones. He nodded slightly as Antonio called out to him. Antonio started running in his direction.

Antonio began to dig his friend out. He threw one rock after another to the side.

He was trying to move as quickly as possible because he could see the color draining from Orsini's face. Both of his eyes were already closed. The debris had crushed his lower body up to his spine, and the dented steel armor had been thrust into his flesh. Even after he had been freed from the mountain of rubble, his blood stained the ground beneath him in widening pools of darkness.

Antonio felt completely helpless. He could only think to remove the armor that was squeezing his friend's body. Orsini was still breathing after Antonio had stripped the armor off both his lower and upper body, but the end seemed near. Antonio removed Orsini's helmet and held his head, surrounded by flaxen hair, delicately with both arms. His friend opened his eyes for an instant and noticed he was being watched. The left side of his mouth twisted slightly into the lopsided smile that ever adorned his face. To those who knew him it was the expression of his boundless kindness; to those who misread him it was a mocking smirk. It was the expression the knight from Rome wore as he died with a shudder, at the age of twenty-five.

Battle cries raised by both sides disrupted the temporary calm. Antonio softly lowered his friend's head and brandished his sword in the direction of the enemy troops. For the first time in the nearly five months of fighting, he actually felt rage well up within him— against the Turks, and against fate itself.

The fierce attack ended as the sun went down. The Turkish army receded like the tide, leaving their many dead just as they were. The bodies of the Turkish soldiers on the ramparts were thrown into the moat. The defenders carried their own dead into the city. The bodies of the slain knights were washed by their valets, dressed in their knightly uniforms, and laid out in a row in the Church of St. John. The procedure was always the same. After the archbishop performed mass, the dead would be interred in the crypt underneath the floor of the church. Every knight who could be spared attended the funeral mass. Antonio was among those who stood surrounding the bodies spread out on the floor.

He wasn't listening to the archbishop's voice intoning prayers. He only stared at Orsini's dead body three feet away from him. Orsini's lips, which had always radiated a faintly rosy glow, were now pale. Yet Antonio couldn't help feeling that the rosy glow was slowly returning right before his eyes.

Antonio thought back to the time he had been in the hospital. One night, he had been in a fitful, feverish sleep when suddenly he felt something brush against his neck. Fearful that whatever it was would stop if he roused from his shallow slumber, Antonio allowed it to continue. He knew who it was. Or rather, he hoped it was a certain person, and he had no desire to budge.

Orsini's lips lingered on Antonio's neck, moved down to his chest, and then pulled away. At that moment, Antonio tried to speak. Before the words could get out, they were stifled by a passionate kiss. From that day on, the affection between the two young men, one twenty and the other twenty-five, only deepened. It was Antonio's first experience of that beautiful aspect of life.

Antonio stood in the church clutching something tightly in his left hand. He had secretly removed it from Orsini's neck while the Roman's valet had been washing the body. It was a lady's crucifix. Without a doubt, Antonio was the only one among their colleagues who knew that Orsini never took it off. The small crucifix, encrusted with two rows of small rubies that formed a cross, was a memento that Orsini's mother had given him when she'd seen him off to Rhodes. He had been twenty, and she had died less than two years later. Antonio hadn't stolen the crucifix for himself; there was a certain person to whom he intended to deliver it.

After the interment, Antonio did not return to the residence of the Italian knights. He instead went alone along a side street that ran beside the Church of St. John down to the city below. The door of Orsini's house was tightly shut. It didn't appear that anyone was home. Nevertheless, Antonio forcefully rapped the iron ring hanging from the door. A short while later, the door was pushed open from inside and a Greek woman stood before him. Antonio could sense from the oppressive weight in the air that she already knew about Orsini's death. Orsini's valet had probably told her. The hard expression on the Greek woman's face gave no glimpse of what was in her heart. Her eyes also didn't appear to have been softened by tears. Antonio realized then that he, too, hadn't cried at all.

He silently offered her the crucifix in his left hand. She took it, also in silence. Without a word spoken between them, she closed the door.

The Turkish assault came as usual the next day, December 19th. The melee was not limited to the Aragonese section, but also extended to the English and Italian walls. The Grand Master took command on the front line of combat, completely unscathed. People began to believe he was graced with God's special protection.

On the Italian side, the enemy concentrated its attack on the Fort del Carretto. Both sides fought using only their swords. After about three hours of intense fighting, the knights noticed a single armored figure blocking the path from the outer wall to the bottom of the tower. A crowd of enemy soldiers was about to over-whelm him.

This was clearly a suicidal thing to do, but there was no way to call him back. The doors at the base of the fort had been tightly secured, and nobody understood how he had exited. The artillery barrage was so loud that their voices couldn't be heard by the knight anyway. They didn't know who it was.

It wasn't long before Turkish soldiers encircled the knight, who wielded a spear. It danced in the air as the enemy rushed him. The men atop the tower instinctively closed their eyes. When the mass of Turkish soldiers dispersed, an armored body lay motionless on the ground.

That day the signal for the Turkish army's retreat sounded unusually early, just after noon. Almost as soon as the enemy had withdrawn, the knights defending the Italian wall impatiently unbolted the gate and flocked to the fallen knight. When Antonio and another picked him up from either side, the dead knight's helm fell to the ground. Seeing the face that was revealed, they all froze. Underneath a thick bundle of black hair was the unmistakable face of a woman. Antonio immediately recognized her. The other knights seemed to recognize her as well, but nobody said a word. As they started to remove the heavy breastplate, a small ruby crucifix spilled out.

Surrendering the Fortress

That evening the Grand Master handed down his decision to surrender the fortress and accept the sultan's conditions. The decision was communicated to the Turkish camp.

One knight and two representatives of the civilian population entered the Turkish camp on December 20th to confirm the agreement. The Turks halted their attacks, and their soldiers busily removed the bodies of their dead from the moat. No shots were fired at them from the ramparts.

Both armies agreed to a tentative three-day truce on December 21st. In order to guarantee the truce, the defenders sent twenty-five knights and an equal number of commoners to stay in the Turkish camp. From the Turkish side, four hundred Janissaries laid down their arms before being taken into the city.

As before, the negotiations were conducted in Ahmed Pasha's tent. Two knights and two townsfolk represented the defenders. Once the sultan made clear that he had no desire to withdraw any of the previously offered conditions, the negotiations were concluded without further ado. The surrender document was signed in Ahmed Pasha's tent. Ahmed Pasha signed for the Turks, and the executed Dal Mare's successor, a knight from Auvergne who had been appointed Lieutenant Grand Master, signed for the defenders. The agreement was dated December 25th.

That evening, though, trouble visited the city of Rhodes. The four hundred Janissaries in the city had begun looting some of the commoners' homes. The Janissaries may have been disarmed, but they were still four hundred elite warriors of the Turkish army. The people of the city felt menaced, regardless of the absence of weapons. The Grand Master didn't address the situation by sending in his knights. He instead appealed directly to the sultan, saying that the treaty had been violated. The sultan ordered the immediate recall of the Janissaries. As the Turkish soldiers departed the fortress, the twenty-five knights and twenty-five Rhodians returned into the walled city. During the night, the Turkish army withdrew and pitched their tents, as promised, at a location one mile from the city.

On the morning of December 26th, Ahmed Pasha's envoy secretly visited the Grand Master's residence. He carried an invitation for Grand Master L'Isle-Adam to visit the sultan. L'Isle-Adam accepted.

That afternoon, encased formally in armor shining silver from head to toe, he rode his mount over the stone bridge spanning the Gate d'Amboise moat toward the Turkish camp. Behind the Grand Master, also on horseback, followed the young French knight La Vallette carrying the great battle flag of the Order of the Knights of St. John, a white cross on a field of red. Behind him rode in no less formal attire those knights who served as commanders of the eight residences, their young lieutenants in tow. Antonio was included in this group. A white cross on red was emblazoned on the breastplates of all the knights, and multi-colored feathers attached to the crests of their helms fluttered in the breeze. The red capes hanging from the shoulders of the Grand Master and his troop of eighteen were all embroidered with white crosses and nearly covered the backs of their horses.

The Turkish soldiers greeted this splendid entourage with looks of astonishment. They were stunned that the enemy, who had fought through a five-month siege, could appear so fresh and elegant, so majestic and dignified, as if they had arrived only yesterday from some port in Western Europe. They had expected to see dirty, defeated survivors hanging their heads in exhaustion as they rode in. The Turkish troops instinctively stepped aside for the knights as the entourage passed through toward the sultan's sparkling golden tent.

Ahmed Pasha and Ibrahim, Suleiman's trusted aide, were waiting outside the tent to greet them. The knights dismounted and Ahmed Pasha led them in. The interior of the tent was even larger than they had imagined. There seemed to be a central chamber surrounded by small rooms. Suleiman was sitting in a low Turkish-style chair, luxuriously inlaid with silver, in the middle of the chamber. As soon as he saw the Grand Master enter, he immediately rose to welcome the group.

The Victor and the Vanquished

The twenty-eight-year-old absolute monarch of the Turks was a tall man with a dignified bearing. Collarless Ottoman clothing tended to make one's neck appear longer than it really was, but Suleiman's neck, though perhaps long, was not slender. On top of that, his plain white silk turban was quite heavy, so that with his above-average height, he appeared to have a slightly arched back, which somehow gave him an air of friendliness.

His narrow face was nicely complemented by his multi-layered turban. His large aquiline nose was conspicuous and characteristically Turkish. His Turkish-style moustache, still relatively small due to his youth, made him appear refined rather than stern. His eyes were large and black instead of the Persian almond shape. Moreover, they sparkled with life, revealing warmth and kindness.

His clothing was more luxurious than it was beautiful. His jacket, which trailed to his feet, was made of brocade abundantly stitched with golden thread. The shirt that peeked out of the thick sleeves was green velvet. The buttons fastening this shirt were each crafted out of gold with the most exquisite workmanship imaginable. An emerald the size of an egg gleamed in the middle of his white silk turban.

Antonio was awestruck. He had heard from childhood that the Turks were barbarians, so this was not what he had expected. The young European was about to be dazzled even further by the spectacle that was about to unfold.

Suleiman offered the Grand Master a chair, and sat himself on his own low Turkish-style seat. The knights stood behind the Grand Master, while three of the viziers—Ahmed Pasha, Kazim Pasha, and Piri Pasha—stood to the sultan's left. Ibrahim stood to his right. The discussion was conducted in Greek. One of the knights translated the Grand Master's French into Greek. Most of the Turkish ministers—certainly Ibrahim, who was Greek—seemed to understand Greek. The sultan himself spoke in Greek.

He swore by Allah, the prophet Mohammed, and the Black Stone of Mecca that he would uphold all conditions of the treaty. The knights heard in the infidel's oath the same sincerity they would have sought in a vow by a Christian knight. Furthermore, the young sultan added that if the twelve-day period to prepare for the exodus were insufficient, he would grant them more time. The Grand Master replied that even though he was deeply grateful for the goodwill shown by the offer, he had no desire to extend the reprieve unnecessarily.

Any discussion between victors and vanquished was not something that could continue in a friendly fashion for very long. As the brief discussion came to a close, the sultan calmly looked the Grand Master in the eye and said:

"I have won. Despite that, I cannot help but feel heartfelt sadness that you and your followers, who are so courageous and upright, are being forced from your homes."

L'Isle-Adam was filled with a flood of emotions as he gazed at the young victor, but still could say nothing. Suleiman presented each member of the entourage with a red velvet scroll. The eighteen knights retraced their path through the d'Amboise Gate and returned to the fortress.

On December 29th, Suleiman entered the fortress of Rhodes as he had previously informed the Grand Master he would. An honor guard of one hundred Janissaries surrounded the sultan, who was on horseback. Of his high ministers, only Ibrahim accompanied him as he entered the fortress. The sultan entered through the Koskinou Gate, but he only went as far as the merchant harbor. He made no attempt to enter the district commonly known as the Chateaux, where the Grand Master's Palace and the residences of the knights were located.

Perhaps the expansive sense of security that came from

being master of a great empire, coupled with the compassion of the victorious, made his first entry into the fortress different from that of the usual conqueror. The young sultan had put his own soldiers on notice that any disrespectful treatment of the defeated would be met with severe punishment. His order was obeyed without exception.

They Depart

The work of loading the belongings and freight of those who were leaving gave the merchant harbor an air of activity unseen in the previous six months. Of the commoners, five thousand had decided to join the exodus. Very few among them, however, had decided where they would settle. The knights were in the same predicament.

They needed at least fifty ships to carry five thousand people and their baggage. Rhodes, which had been under siege for six months, did not harbor that many ships at the moment. In the end, vessels provided by the Turkish navy were necessary for the people and freight that couldn't be accommodated by the ships from Genoa, Venice, and Marseilles. The Turks had promised to transport them only as far as Venetian-controlled Crete. Everyone wanted to board ships belonging to Rhodes or Western Europe, creating a congested rush in the merchant harbor.

The military harbor was equally congested, but for a

different reason. The knights had few accoutrements so loading them didn't take much time at all. Rather, since it was important to the knights, as warriors, that everybody know they had surrendered with honor, they needed to load all of their weapons and gear. Their cannons were the only things the Turks would not allow them to take along.

There were also the holy relics collected by the order from the time they had been active in Palestine. The knights and the relics had shared a common fate ever since they had been forced to abandon Palestine and make a new home in Rhodes. Like the knights, the relics would have no safe place to rest until their next home had been found and secured. The treasures of the Order of the Knights of St. John included the right hand of St. John, which was kept in a magnificent silver container; a shard from the cross upon which Christ was crucified; two thorns from the crown that Christ was made to wear before his crucifixion; the mummified body of St. Euphemia; and many blessed and sacred ancient icons. These relics were placed in the cabin of the *Santa Maria*, the flagship that the Grand Master would be boarding.

The knights began boarding the wounded after having loaded the treasures, weapons, battle flags, and accoutrements. Those who could walk leaned on the shoulders of their comrades. Those who could not were loaded onto the ships on stretchers. All preparations were completed on the final day of December. They were to set sail the following day, the first of January.

The Grand Master visited the sultan's tent on the morning of departure to offer parting formalities. Suleiman had prepared official travel documents that guaranteed all who were leaving free and safe passage throughout the Ottoman Empire. The Grand Master and Sultan Suleiman spent more time together that day than they had previously. L'Isle-Adam later described the sultan as "a knight in the truest sense of the word."

The wind stung the skin on January 1, 1523, but the skies were clear and blue. Snow must have capped the highest peaks of the mountain range that served as the backbone of the Isle of Rhodes.

Knights had begun boarding their ships in the military harbor. The merchant harbor was cluttered with ships flying Genoese, Venetian, and French flags; the first wave of departing residents had been waiting since the previous evening aboard a total of eleven ships. The remaining refugees would board Turkish ships as soon as they had completed their preparations, and then follow behind the ships that were leaving that day. Reluctant farewells were exchanged on the docks between those aboard and those who had come to see them off.

Suleiman was considerate enough to ensure that there was no Turkish naval presence at the military harbor. Very few people had come to see the knights off, since members of the order had no family or relatives on the island. The knights silently boarded the fully readied ships. Antonio dragged his right leg. The Turkish soldier's dagger had struck bone, and even though the wound was completely healed, he had to walk with a limp. All the knights whose own legs would carry them wore the formal attire of the Order of the Knights of St. John even on this day.

The twenty-five ships waiting to depart from the docks of the military harbor consisted of one large transport vessel, fourteen small single-mast galleys, three large two-mast galleys, and seven three-mast fighting frigates outfitted with both square and triangular sails. This was the convoy by which the Knights would leave the island. The size of the fleet was truly meager considering that this was the navy that had dominated the region's seas for two hundred years. It was true that they had ceded a number of ships to the commoners for their departure and that another ten ships were considered unsafe. Since no one could predict how these would hold up on a long voyage, in the end, they had to leave them behind in the shipyard.

The flagship *Santa Maria* that provided the berths of the Grand Master and the archbishop was a three-mast fighting frigate built noticeably larger than the six other similar ships. Captained by the English knight Sir William Weston, it led the convoy out of the harbor. One by one, the other ships followed in its wake. All the church bells began to chime in unison from within the fortress walls of Rhodes, rung by people unknown.

A white cross on a triangular field of red, the battle

flag of the Order of the Knights of St. John, flapped in the breeze atop the mast of every ship leaving the harbor. The knights' shields, also with white crosses on red, were arrayed on the sides of each ship, and behind these stood the knights holding their lances. This was the custom of the order when heading into battle. The windmills stretching along the top of the breakwaters rattled as the ships passed.

As the flagship led the convoy past the Fort of St. Nicholas, which secured the military harbor, cannon fire could be heard echoing from the fortress. Suleiman had ordered a salute. The knights were speechless as they stared back at the Isle of Rhodes receding in the distance. The decks were completely silent.

They were leaving the ancient isle of blossoming roses, which had been their home for two hundred years. The bugler on the *Santa Maria*'s stern started to play in response to the chime of the bells and the cannon salute. The bugle's plaintive tone rose higher and higher as it coursed over the surface of the sea.

Antonio, the new recruit who had been on the island for less than a year, and Martinengo, who was not even a knight, shared the others' heartfelt pain. Nobody could take his eyes off the Isle of Rhodes as it disappeared over the horizon.

The convoy's first destination was the port of Canea, on the western shore of Crete. The Venetian Republic, which controlled Crete, had offered a number of buildings in Canea as a temporary shelter for the refugees. The Venetians would also permit the sick and injured to stay in the local hospital. Where the knights would go after that was still undecided.

At last, that "nest of Christian vipers" had been totally cleaned out which had been built so boldly, small as it was, within the inner courtyard of the Ottoman Empire. Even though this success came at a tremendous sacrifice, the Turks believed that the reward was far greater. The trip from the imperial capital of Constantinople to faraway Syria or Egypt, as well as the pilgrimage to Mecca on the Arabian peninsula, could now be undertaken without fear of an attack en route.

Yet, one young and particularly venomous "viper" had been allowed to escape thanks to a display of chivalrous spirit superior to any among the French aristocracy. That fact, though, went unnoticed at the time by the twenty-eight-year-old victor.

Epilogue

Wandering Years

Grand Master L'Isle-Adam began demonstrating a genuine talent for leading an organization precisely after the Order of the Knights of St. John became a band of refugees.

The Western Europeans who had temporarily settled in Canea gradually began to leave for their respective homelands, while most of the Greeks from Rhodes settled on Crete or other islands in the Aegean Sea. Thus the knights were spared the ordeal that befell the Venetian Republic when the Turks conquered Albania and a home had to be procured immediately for the resulting flood of refugees. The only problem was that the order needed to find a state that would accept them as an organization and not merely as individual knights.

At first the Grand Master was preoccupied by thoughts of raising a joint force from the armies of Western Europe and using it to retake Rhodes. During their three months on Crete he sent emissaries to Rome tirelessly to plead for the pope's assistance. Pope Adrian VI was a sincere man but had no political power; he needed to get the College of Cardinals to rule on the matter. One of the cardinals, Medici, was a member of the order; he had some political power but was anything but sincere. Refusing to cooperate with the reigning pope, he remained in Florence from where he sent back vague replies to the Grand Master's pleas.

In April, the order moved to Messina in Sicily. Crete

belonged to the Venetian Republic, and the Venetians, who took a soft line toward the Turks, had no desire to keep the knights, perennial hard-liners, within their territory for too long.

But the Knights' stay on Messina was also brief. Messina was controlled by the King of Spain. The Governor of Sicily, a subject of the king, was opposed to the Knights' establishing their base there. The order was forced into a vagabond existence, traveling along with their holy relics and battle flags to Genoa, Nice, and Viterbo in central Italy. L'Isle-Adam even visited the palaces of the ruling monarchs of Western Europe during this time, tireless in his call for a crusade to restore Rhodes. The monarchs, though, never came to share his enthusiasm for the project.

Five years after the fall of Rhodes, in 1527, a major incident occurred. The army of the Holy Roman Emperor Charles, King of Spain, attacked Rome, the seat of the pope, and burned and plundered the city. Rome was manifestly in no position to contemplate anything like a crusade against the Turks. The knights of the order realized that they had to abandon any hope of recovering their home on Rhodes. They settled on a strategy of appealing to the monarchs of Western Europe for a new base. They petitioned for Sicily, then for a section of Sardinia, then for a part of Corsica; as a last resort, they even considered the island of Elba. None of these plans ever materialized.

The Knights of Malta

As it happened, in 1530, Charles seemed to remember that he had three Mediterranean islands in his possession: Malta and two associated isles. He thought it would do to present these to the Knights, and an agreement was reached under which they agreed to present a tribute of one Maltese falcon each year. As long as the order was in charge of Malta, however, the knights were the subjects of the Spanish throne. They were tasked with attacking Tripoli in North Africa.

We see here exactly how Charles intended to make use of the order. His ambition was to rule all of North Africa, including Algeria and Tunisia. He also wanted the knights to protect merchant ships in his territories from the Muslim pirates (also known as the "Barbary pirates") who had set up base there and were terrorizing the entire region. The Ottoman Empire lacked naval power and thus granted the pirates authority over the land and ports of the Barbary Coast in North Africa on the condition that the pirates contribute ships to the Turkish navy in emergencies.

If they established their base on Malta in the Western Mediterranean, the knights could no longer claim to be on the front line against the infidel, as they had been in Rhodes. They would become nothing more than King Charles's watchdogs on Malta, with only pirates as adversaries.

The Grand Master was well aware of this. But if he

refused Malta, there was no telling when or where they could set up a new headquarters. The justification for their continued existence may have been the mere eradication of pirates, but that was still a cause. Acquiring a base and a reason for being was essential if they were to remain an order.

In 1530, eight years after having been chased out of Rhodes, the order completed the move to Malta.

Conditions on the island, however, were enough to send the knights, who were accustomed to the "Ancient Isle of Blossoming Roses," into a state of despair.

The climate was harsh. Virtually the entire island was a barren mountain range, and both the winter cold and the summer heat were unbearable. The island was a forgotten backwater, with a total population barely exceeding ten thousand. Almost all of the residents were illiterate, and the spoken language was a dialect of Arabic owing to the proximity of North Africa and a history of Arab rule some five hundred years earlier. The few among the impoverished masses who formed something like an upper class were the descendants of the Spaniards who ruled Sicily. They could speak a little Spanish, Italian, and French. In short, on Malta, the knights could not expect the warm climate, the greenery, or the lingering fragrance of civilization that had been so abundant on Rhodes.

A number of knights from each unit retired from the order as a result of the move. Their excuse was that, on Malta, the order had lost its original reason for being. Working as Charles's hound was beneath the dignity of these knights. La Vallette, who had used the same reasoning in the council meeting in Rhodes to argue for continued resistance, remained in the order. Perhaps the image of the Turkish victor who was the same age as himself remained engraved in his memory.

Grand Master L'Isle-Adam died on Malta four years after the move. Around then, things were beginning to change on the island.

While there had been buildings on Rhodes dating back to the Byzantine era, on Malta the knights had to build everything from the ground up. Upon first arriving on Rhodes they had used the buildings they'd found, but as the years passed and their ability to raise funds grew, they expanded, remodeled, and refitted in order to construct the strongest fortress in the Mediterranean. Such a feat was nothing more than a dream on Malta, which didn't possess a single ancient or medieval remain. Furthermore, from the Knights' perspective, and indeed according to the common sense of the day, life without some sort of protective fortress was unimaginable. Perhaps the only merit of the barren island of Malta was that it was blessed with many harbors, each carved deeply out of a landscape of jagged boulders. Sufficient work and maintenance could transform them into some of the finest ports in the Mediterranean.

The Knights began fortifying that stretch of land,

which was uninhabited. As before, the planning and supervision was the work of Italian fortress engineers. The Knights decided to make that spot, which was still without a name, their capital. Work on the fortifications was just getting underway when L'Isle-Adam died, but the Grand Masters who succeeded him embraced his vision and poured all their energy into seeing it fulfilled. In 1557, twenty-seven years after the move to Malta, the fortification of the bay was almost half-done. The enterprise involved fortifying all eight peninsulas jutting out into the bay, one at a time. The order wasn't as wealthy during the Malta years as it had been before, so the project couldn't be completed in a short period of time.

The engineer Martinengo, who had left Rhodes along with the Knights, didn't participate in the fortification of Malta. This is not to say that he and the Knights had parted ways. Martinengo, who had to wear a patch over his right eye after his wounding in Rhodes, was knighted by L'Isle-Adam after the order surrendered the fortress. This was of course a reward for his service to the defenders, but it was an unprecedented step actually to knight somebody who didn't have a drop of noble blood. Martinengo was one of the knights who visited Charles's court to negotiate the handover of Malta, evidence that he was active in the order during its years of wandering.

Yet, instead of going to Malta himself, he recommended other engineers who wound up doing the work.

Martinengo had been asked by Charles to stay in Spain and serve as fortress engineer. He was responsible for strengthening the fortress at San Sebastian with bastions at key points, making it the first of its kind in Spain. He later returned to Italy, where he oversaw the expansion and repair of fortresses in Pavia, Genoa, and Naples. He was even sent as far as Antwerp in Holland with another Italian engineer to oversee the planning of that city's defense.

Martinengo died in Venice in 1544. Until a few years prior to his death, he had always believed that his homeland hadn't approved of his unannounced departure for Rhodes. A letter survives that he wrote to his brother, dated October 1522, before Rhodes had surrendered to the Turks. In it, he conveyed his concerns about how the Venetian government interpreted his absence without leave, but also described in detail the Turks' artillery and mine offensives.

Vengeance

In 1557, Jean de la Vallette-Parisot was elected Grand Master of the Order of the Knights of St. John, replacing his deceased predecessor. At Rhodes he had been in his late twenties but was sixty-three at the time of his election. People said of him that he was "unrivalled in purity, bearer of the unadulterated soul of Gascony." Even in his sixties he had a body like tempered steel and an unflagging spirit. He was the only man who was still determined to eradicate the infidels, especially the Turks who had expelled the order from Rhodes.

Eight years after becoming Grand Master, he finally had the opportunity to act on that determination. In 1565, the Turks sent a large force to conquer Malta. Suleiman, the same man La Vallette had met on Rhodes, was still sultan. Now known as "Suleiman the Magnificent," he was over seventy years old and rarely set foot on a battlefield. He had assigned the siege of Malta to a subordinate; he himself never stepped outside the walls of his tulip-bedecked Topkapi Palace in Constantinople. La Vallette was the same age as the sultan, yet he assumed direct leadership of his forces. Now, forty-three years after the Ottoman Empire's victory over the Knights of St. John at Rhodes, there was to be a rematch.

In the spring of 1565, the Turkish army left Constantinople for Malta. The reported figure of two thousand ships of various sizes may have been exaggerated, but whatever the case may be, it was the first time that the Mediterranean Sea had seen such a great fleet, one carrying over 50,000 soldiers. The commander of the expedition was Mustafa Pasha, the same man whose all-out attack during the siege of Rhodes had failed and who had been demoted and sent to Syria. Subsequent successes in campaigns against Persia and Hungary had allowed him to be restored to his former rank. Suleiman appointed him supreme commander in this offensive to give him a chance to extract revenge against the Order of St. John for his previous humiliation.

The defenders had a contingent of 540 knights, one thousand Spanish soldiers, and a total of four thousand mercenaries and Maltese residents. This force was approximately the same size as that which had defended Rhodes. La Vallette, who had been twenty-eight during the siege of Rhodes, was now seventy-one.

The Turks, however, faced a number of disadvantages at Malta that hadn't existed at Rhodes, in addition to the sultan's absence.

First, the aggressors possessed only half the manpower they had wielded on Rhodes. In addition, on Malta they couldn't expect an equally large reserve to be sent from Syria and Egypt. Second, the distance from Constantinople to Malta was twice as much as that from Constantinople to Rhodes. Unlike the previous campaign, they couldn't travel across Asia Minor, which they controlled, and then take a short fifty-kilometer hop from Marmaris to Rhodes. This time the entire journey was by sea, a distance of over 1600 kilometers. This would have been difficult enough only with soldiers, but they also had to carry all of their supplies: cannons, cannonballs, gunpowder, even food stores. And they had to do it all in one trip. The previous time they had had the luxury of a continuous stream of supply ships shuttling back and forth between Marmaris and Rhodes. It would not be the case during the Malta campaign.

North Africa, of course, was part of the Ottoman Empire. The sultan, however, had entrusted the territory to Barbary pirates so it was not under his direct control. Thus it was impossible to construct a supply line to Malta from Tunisia, the nearest point in North Africa, as they had from Asia Minor to Rhodes.

Third, the knights had fortified a number of peninsulas as a provision for Malta's defense. The Turks were unable to concentrate all their forces in one location as they had on Rhodes. The defenders had divided their forces, and the attackers were obligated to do likewise, even though the Turks were not masters of tactical finesse. The Turkish army was built for the massive application of force, so this dispersion of focus hurt the Turks more than the Order of St. John. La Vallette discovered that fighting on twelve separate defensive fronts maximized their advantage.

Fourth, Malta was close to Sicily, which in that day was under Spanish rule. This was the reign of Charles's son Philip II, who couldn't have been pleased that the Turkish army was moving into areas bordering on his own territory. Once the Ottoman Empire decided to invade Malta, the Grand Master appealed to the Spanish king to send reinforcements. The king responded with a promise to send 16,000 men. La Vallette said he would only believe the monarch's words when he actually saw the soldiers, but in fact nobody had more to lose from a Turkish victory in Malta than the King of Spain.

The fighting began in mid-May, after the Turks had landed the last of their army. The attacks were ratcheted up to a ferocity unseen even on Rhodes. The defenders' greatest advantage, however, lay in the fact that no civilians were found in the fortresses. The dispersed fortresses were occupied only by combatants, who were barricaded inside. No matter how bad things got for the defenders, they didn't have to worry about changes of heart among the common people. Whether the defenders held together or not depended solely on the will of the Grand Master, and La Vallette was an iron-willed man.

Of course there was the fact that if the Knights lost Malta, they had nowhere else to go. La Vallette completely ignored Mustafa Pasha's peace overtures, which included even better terms than those at Rhodes. The "vipers" who had lost their great nest on the Isle of Rhodes surely wanted to sink their poisonous fangs into the ones who had robbed them of it. They would defend their new lair to the end, or die trying. When Mustafa Pasha cut off the head of a captured knight and shot it at them as a cannonball, La Vallette returned fire with the heads of Turkish soldiers.

On September 6th, as the siege approached its fourth month, eight thousand troops arrived, dispatched by the Governor of Sicily. This was only half of what Philip II had promised, but combined with the fact that the siege was going nowhere and had resulted in heavy Turkish losses, it was enough to demoralize the Turkish army and prompt a lifting of the siege. It is said that when the Turks broke camp, they left Malta with only a third of the men with whom they had arrived. Mustafa Pasha, who bore the responsibility for the defeat, was terrified at the thought of the punishment Suleiman had waiting for him, but the sultan was remarkably dispassionate about the whole affair. Perhaps Suleiman and Mustafa were both showing their age.

It is unknown whether Suleiman was aware that the person who deserved the most credit for the defense of Malta was the French knight he had met twice during the siege of Rhodes. If he knew, he may have regretted his own gentlemanly behavior on those earlier occasions. Suleiman the Magnificent died just one year later.

La Vallette lived for another three years. He died in 1568 after spending the final stretch of his life repairing and reinforcing the severely damaged fortress walls, preparing them to withstand the Turks' next attack.

The fortified area surrounding the harbor in due course became the capital of Malta. It was named Valletta and remains so to this day, though the Order of the Knights of St. John left the island after being subdued by Napoleon. Malta became the property of France, and later of England. It is now an independent republic, but the name of the capital remains unchanged.

Another Option

Antonio del Carretto never became a member of the Knights of Malta, as the Order of the Knights of St. John came to be called after it relocated to that island.

He had shared in their "refugee" existence for several years after the Knights' departure from Rhodes, but he then retired from the order. A number of other knights had done the same, besides which Antonio also had the excuse of a lame leg. In any event, the order never asked too many questions in such cases.

Six years after Antonio left Rhodes, his father the marquis died. Antonio's older brother, Giovanni, succeeded him, and his mother Peretta remarried soon thereafter. By that time, Antonio had already relinquished his knighthood and entered a monastery. He had chosen the path of an ordinary monk. Although only fragments remain concerning his life in the monastery, he seems to have written an account of the defense of Rhodes. It was preserved at his monastery near Genoa, but Antonio later left that monastery and never returned.

His mother's remarriage made news not only in the household of the late Marquis del Carretto, but indeed throughout Genoa, because her new husband was the famous Admiral Andrea Doria. The Genoese aristocrat Doria was not an admiral of the Genoese navy, but rather the captain of a group of seafaring mercenaries. He and his sailors made their living by fighting for any ruler with the money to hire them. At that time, mercenary captains on land were not uncommon, but he was the best one on sea. One minute he was working for the pope, and the next it was the King of France. When he was no longer happy with the French king's terms of employment, he went to work for his rival, the King of Spain. He was over sixty when he married Peretta, but he was a hale man who wouldn't die until he was ninety-four. He was nicknamed the "Lone Wolf," or more pejoratively, "The Shark," by the Spanish and the French, both of whom lacked experience in naval warfare. Doria served their needs and profited by supplying a service much in demand. He was a shrewd man and truly adept at turning a profit, even if that meant bargaining with Muslim pirates.

He had accumulated enormous wealth in his years as a mercenary. His relationships with powerful employers afforded him a level of political influence unrivaled by any other Genoese. In other words, Antonio's mother Peretta chose a highly accomplished man as her second husband. The marriage occasioned much gossip, but Antonio himself wasn't inclined to think ill of his mother's choice. Sensual women love men who wield power. Antonio himself hadn't chosen the path of wealth and power, but he wasn't narrow-minded enough to be critical of those who did. His mother was a woman who enjoyed life with her entire being. Antonio had no trouble believing that she actually loved that crafty old shark of the Mediterranean, and the idea brought a wry smile to his face.

Antonio chose a different life from his brother Marco, who became Andrea Doria's adopted son and embarked on his own career as a fighting sea captain. After Antonio left the monastery, he traveled to the Muslim countries of North Africa. He went first to Tunisia, traveling as an ordinary monk with only the robes on his back.

His mission was not to spread the Gospel of Christ. He wanted only to see to the welfare of the Christian prisoners in Muslim lands. The Barbary pirates' strongholds were in Tunisia and Algeria; their prisoners were held in detention camps called "baths." The practice was to hold prisoners until a ransom was paid and they were set free; if no ransom came, they were sold into slavery. Prisoners for whom no buyer could be found lived out their lives in the "baths." Antonio joined a European religious order that was set up to deliver ransoms, to collect funds for those unable to pay, and to care for the sick and injured among the incarcerated.

The date of his death is unknown. He had given up his name upon becoming a knight, and died that way, in anonymity. In his final days Antonio del Carretto was known simply as "the lame monk."

The Order of the Knights of St. John Today

In June of 1798 the Order of the Knights of St. John was expelled from Malta by Napoleon, en route on his Egyptian expedition. Napoleon decided to subjugate the island almost on a whim, but the knights wound up surrendering without any resistance.

On June 12th, Napoleon himself entered the capital of Valletta. Even he couldn't but be awed by the daunting and marvelous fortress city. He later wrote: "Malta would have fallen in twenty-fours at most. The walls certainly could have endured our bombardment, but the knights manning them were lacking in spirit."

The island of Malta became the property of England in 1814 after Napoleon's downfall. Much later it was to gain independence as a result of the Second World War. Nevertheless, Malta's crest is still emblazoned with the eight-cornered cross of the Order of the Knights of St. John, and the capital is still called Valletta. The fortress completed by the order still serves as a magnificent naval base, one that, as of this writing, is eagerly coveted by NATO, the Soviet Union, and Libya.

Their expulsion by Napoleon marked the third time since the Crusades that the Knights were forced to become refugees. After leaving Malta they spent some time in Moscow. For some reason the tsar had decided to become the order's protector, even before the fall of Malta. The Knights, however, kept their headquarters in Catania, Sicily. In 1826 they moved it to Ferarra in northern Italy. Several years later, they moved again, to Rome, after a member of the order donated the site of their new headquarters, a building in central Rome. The headquarters of the Order of the Knights of St. John is there even today, side by side with designer boutiques on the Via Condotti, one of Rome's most fashionable avenues. Like the Vatican, the order is a sovereign entity right in the center of Italy. It issues its own license plates and prints its own postage stamps, which can be used to mail letters from the headquarters to a limited number of countries.

The present Grand Master is the seventy-seventh in the line and has eight thousand knights under him. Most of them are married, as no one enforces the vows of poverty, obedience, and chastity any longer. It is important to note, however, that the order (which today goes under the official name Sovereign Military Hospitaller Order of St. John of Jerusalem of Rhodes and of Malta) doesn't simply survive as a curiosity. It continues to be an active organization. While the Crusaders have disappeared, the order's other responsibility, the practice of medicine, still remains. A keen eye will notice that their peculiarly shaped white cross on a field of red can be found even today affixed to hospitals, research centers, and ambulances. They still live in residences divided by nation of origin. They are the knights of our century.

That said, they are no longer required to be blue-bloods. The prerequisite of noble birth probably lost its meaning as the wars against the infidel came to an end. The Order of the Knights of St. John, established nine hundred years ago in Jerusalem by a merchant from Amalfi, has returned to its founding mission.